Dark Spots in the Tall Grass

Travelling Moments
in Lesotho and South Africa

Judi King

Dark Spots in the Tall Grass

Travelling Moments in
Lesotho and South Africa

Judi King

Bibliographic information available from Deutsche Nationalbibliothek/German National Library (www.dnb.de)

Printed and published by BoD – Books on Demand, Norderstedt, Germany

ISBN: 978-3-756-840403

Horns Above My Head

Never had I dreamt of visiting Africa. Yet, since the days of my childhood I had been passing below the horns of an African buffalo that towered over the entrance gate to my family home. Exposed to the elements for decades, they became brittle and disintegrated years ago.

They were not forgotten. Those imposing horns were my introduction to South Africa that I visited on three occasions. An excursion to the Kingdom of Lesotho was an added appeal to travel.

We saw a variety of horns, wide ones, straight ones, spiralled ones, and all still where they ought to be.

With animals, plants and landscapes taking centre stage, the dramatic background of European intrusion into the region was still notable in many places.

Turning my brief diary into a travel narrative, by way of complementing my own experience of the country, I added references to memoirs, journals and reports of officials, scientists, adventurers, and explorers visiting the area or stationed there long before me.

While my first glimpse of an unknown country were mysterious buffalo horns, I returned with a cheerful hippo and a wooden elephant that are now happily grunting and trumpeting in the library in my house.

The lionesses I faced, I left in the bush though.

'Pleasure and interest can be obtained from the observation and study of wild animals'

Dogs, Elephants and Herdboys:
Pretoria, Kruger National Park
and Lesotho

Out of the blue, my husband Peter asked what I thought about a little trip to the country where my buffalo once might have roamed.

'Would you like to find out where he lived, before someone showed up with a heavy calibre rifle?'

'Well, it would not help him very much now. But since he looked down at me for years, I think I owe it to him.'

Kruger National Park was to be our main destination with a brief excursion to Lesotho on the side. Though only a short visit to South Africa, we were to gain first impressions of the country and an introduction to its wildlife. Details were planned by our friend in Pretoria.

I hoped to encounter a buffalo with his horns still gracing his head. What I did not anticipate, however, was a lioness passing us a few centimetres away.

Pretoria

Arriving in Johannesburg from London after a 10 1/2 hour flight on Virgin Atlantic on a Sunday morning in mid April, bright sunlight and warm temperatures helped us to face the day cheerfully after a night without much sleep. At the arrivals hall we were met by William to take us to his house in Pretoria, a trip of forty-five minutes.

The city of Pretoria is the administrative capital of the Republic of South Africa. Since 1910, with the founding of the Union of South Africa, the city is one of the three capital cities of the country. Situated in Gauteng, it is one of the four provinces the former Transvaal was divided into after the end of apartheid in 1994; the other three provinces are Mpumalanga, Limpopo and Northwest respectively. Like many places in South Africa, besides native roots, it has a European history.

The Boer background of the city

Capital of the Transvaal or The South African Republic in 1860, Pretoria was founded in 1855 by Marthinus Wessel Pretorius, also the republic's first president. It was named in honour of his father Andries Pretorius, one of the leaders of the Voortrekker, the pioneer Boer settlers, who left the Cape Colony to move farther inland after the 1830s.

Intending to distance themselves from British Imperial rule after Britain took over The Cape from the Dutch in 1806, at various times groups of Boers trekked east and north-east, extending the boundaries of white settlement. Pushing out of the Cape north-east beyond the Vaal River, the Boer families travelled through areas which had seen unrest for years.

Prolonged drought and famine in the early 1800s and again in the 1820s as well as a devastating cattle disease in 1817 had destabilised many regions and induced peoples to move in search of food, water and new pastures. Native groups and the Boers were migrating through regions which had been used by local tribes, thus disrupting and unbalancing large areas, fighting and killing each other in the process. Trekking along, forming temporary alliances with some chiefs and dispossessing others, the various Boer parties established a number of settlements, one of which became Pretoria.

Security on eight paws

Our friend was living in one of the suburbs, where homes were protected by security walls, guarded by ferocious dogs and monitored by high-tech cameras. Like other properties in the neighbourhood, William's house and garden were enclosed by a 1.80m high steel perimeter fence and patrolled by two fearsome looking dogs. The iron driveway gate was remote-controlled to make sure the car got in and out very quickly, shutting immediately after we had passed. Thus, time for any intruder or hijacker to sneak in was kept to a minimum. South Africa was a country where people had to lock themselves in to be safe.

While William showed us around his pleasant house and lush garden, the two dogs trailed us curious to discover their master's new companions. A respect-inducing German shepherd and a terror-instilling Doberman with razor sharp teeth, they seemed to be quite intimidating. I thought that these two would send anyone with designs on entering the property uninvited, even a well seasoned thief, into a bone-rattling fright and make him fall off the fence in a major panic. Suspicious of any strangers, sentry dogs like those two would normally attack anyone entering their patch. Assured by our friend that we were acceptable, threatening behaviour was left for bad characters. In fact, both were very friendly and craved for attention, just wanting to be patted and talked to.

'Anyone being welcomed by you with bare teeth would not be tempted to think that you two are rather endearing creatures, would they?'

The Doberman snarled, craftiness in his face.

'So, you are deceiving the intruders, only to snap at their bottoms and ankles and legs.'

The German shepherd grinned, his eyes blinking cunningly.

Heads cocked and tails wagging, both looked at me and then sat down by my side, one right, one left. Friends not foes.

Fortunately, burglars and robbers did not know the soft side of those reputedly vicious guard dogs. Except if the intruders were Crocodile Dundee scaling the fence, they could easily turn savage dogs into tame pets, like buffalos standing on the red sand track in the outback.

Sights of the town

Mid afternoon we were taken on a short sightseeing trip around Pretoria. Since the city has one of the highest crime rates in the world and the likelihood of falling victims to muggers was quite real, we were not supposed to explore the town centre on foot. On a brief drive through town, with car doors locked, William showed us a few points of interest, which had not been there when a famous Englishman visited in the late 19th century. Unlike him, I saw what he assumed the town to evolve into.

When the Victorian novelist Anthony Trollope was there in 1877, the town, still in its infancy, had unpaved and potholed streets with small one-storey houses, and many people were rather destitute. "And yet in spite of the mud, in spite of the brandy bottles, in spite of the ubiquitous rags Pretoria is both picturesque and promising." He saw some improvements being made and envisaged the place one day "likely to be a distinguished success." [1] His prediction proved correct. Today, the city is well laid-out with wide roads, shopping malls, office blocks, government buildings, sports facilities, churches, parks, museums, squares and a number of public spaces.

Pretoria is a place of big and small businesses, with its industrial areas at the periphery. While driving through the central commercial district we saw all sorts of shops, eateries, banks and some tall corporate buildings. There was plenty of traffic on the streets and on the pavements, picturesque it was not but very busy.

---

[1] South Africa, vol II, p51, 50.

In the quieter Church Square on a pedestal sat the statue of Paul Kruger, four times president of the Transvaal or the South African Republic between 1883 and 1902. The space was surrounded by imposing public buildings like the Palace of Justice, which came to international prominence in the recent past. It was here, in 1964, that Nelson Mandela was charged with conspiracy and sent to prison for over twenty-five years. The trial is described in part seven of his autobiography *Long walk to Freedom.*

Thirty years later, in May 1994, not far away from the place of his sentencing, Mr Mandela was inaugurated as the new president of the Republic of South Africa at the Unions Buildings, seat of the government and the president's offices. Their generous park with terraced gardens, lawns and plants, monuments and memorials was a good place for looking across the city. We took a brief walk through the beautifully laid out grounds, which in the 1850s had been the farm of Marthinus Wessel Pretorius.

Seated on benches in the warm sunshine we talked about the latest developments in our lives. Last time we had met was quite a while ago at a conference in Scandinavia, so there was a lot of catching up to do. The most important topic, however, was a brief visit to the Kruger National Park in a few days' time. William had it all planned. But not only that. Since he knew that we were interested in animals and plants, he had arranged to go to an animal sanctuary in the region and the botanical gardens of the city before setting off for Kruger.

Before we fell into bed, we were treated to a traditional Afrikaaner meal of papp, beef and salad. Barbecued meat was accompanied by a stiff porridge made from maize flour and a bowl of crisp green leaves.

The dogs were on duty outside and did not like that in the least.

Where the cheetah runs to the restrooms

Next morning, William took us to the de Wildt Cheetah Centre, also known as The Ann van Dyk Cheetah Centre, on the R513 to Madibeng near Brits in the foothills of the Magaliesberg Mountain Range, 50km from Pretoria.

The wildlife sanctuary has been established in 1971 to conserve, breed and reintroduce endangered species, in particular the cheetah and the king cheetah. Reduced in numbers by hunting, poisoning and indiscriminate killing for nearly a century, their survival has been ensured for the time being. On account of the organisation's conservation and breeding success, cheetahs were no longer on the list of endangered animals as they had been in the 1960s. Besides caring for the fastest of the big cats, de Wildt was also a safe place for other animals at risk such as wild dogs, brown hyenas and vultures.

After a brief introduction to the organisation and their conservation projects, we climbed into an open vehicle for a tour around the centre together with a dozen other people. Visitors were not allowed to walk around on their own. While driving along the enclosures, we were briefed on their temporary and long-term residents.

Recyclers, pest controllers, dancers

A congregation of Cape vultures was assembled in a large aviary. Their bills were black, head and neck were bald except for a compact white ruff. Their body feathers were of cream and sand colour with a dark tail. Considering their business, they looked very stylish. You need a good amount of poise going around breaking bones and pulling guts from a blood-dripping carcass, dressed in smart beige-coloured trousers. Minding their ruined finery after the feast, vultures are in the habit of bathing after a feeding session. A beak covered in blood would not go well with a chic outfit.

Unfortunately, their flamboyance does not help them very much. The huge birds have become one of the most threatened species of southern Africa. The scavengers are essential to a healthy ecosystem, as they are able to spot dead animals within half an hour and dispose of them efficiently. Nothing much is left of a carcass they have dismantled, thus they are cleaning up nature. Disregarding their usefulness, the vultures are in serious danger by persecution, electrocution, poisoning as well as by shortage of carrion and loss of foraging habitat. With the result that their numbers are declining at an alarming rate in Africa.

Not only vultures are threatened by poisoning, owls are also killed that way, and their numbers are reduced by parasitic infections. They too are beneficial, since they feed on rodents and large insects as well as small reptiles, thus removing vermin. Nearby, a few beautiful large owls were residing in a spacious aviary dotted with medium sized trees and shrubs. They were spotted eagle-owls with distinct small ear tufts. Their plumage was mainly of an elegant grey-brown colour. Their faces were white with grey bars and yellow eyes. One or two were sitting tight and motionlessly on the ground, some were roosting up in the branches.

What was on their minds being gazed at all day, I wondered. Had they asked me what I thought about them, I would have told them how adorable they were.

Two dashing crowned cranes, resplendent with their distinctive golden feathery crest were strolling in the tall grass. While their feet, legs and bill were black, their eyes were pale blue. Their cheeks were white and the throat had a red pendant wattle. Their plumage had areas of white, grey, black and chestnut brown feathers.

They are known for the elaborate dancing routine during courtship. They hunt for reptiles or insects but also eat grasses and cereal crops which enrages the farmers. Their numbers are declining because of loss of wetland habitat, overgrazing, pollution with pesticides and illegal removal of their eggs in the wild for commercial reasons. Strikingly beautiful birds, they are captured and sold to wealthy individuals who are using them as a status symbol.

Since the tall birds were not kept in an aviary, we assumed they were just visiting, calling on the neighbours for a morning chat.

Stalkers, pouncers, hunters

They probably would not be too keen to meet one of the next residents we saw, predator cats. Also called desert or African lynx, the caracal is a small cat of about 40cm in height with a dense short yellowish-brown coat. It has black lines in its face and long narrow pointed ears with distinct long black tufts on the tip. A nocturnal hunter with a long athletic slender body, long legs and a long tail, the animal is adept at climbing trees. This is a skilled stalker preying on rodents or other small mammals, even catching low-flying birds by leaping up into the air. It can mainly be found in dry savannah and scrub country. Since significant numbers are being killed by farmers on account of their taking domestic livestock, the caracal has become rare in South Africa.

The serval, called tierboskat in Afrikaans, was another pretty cat of about 60cm shoulder height. Its pale yellowish coat was marked with black spots, it had a slim body with long legs and big ears. Preferably hunting in long grass country, a serval leaps in the air before pouncing on its prey, primarily rodents. The main threat to the animals is the loss of wetland and grassland. They are also killed by farmers, though they do not attack livestock.

Only eating fresh and recent kills, a couple of young cheetahs were just about to be fed with horse meat or chicken. We watched them at close range and could clearly see the tear-marks in their faces.

We were also introduced to the beautiful king cheetah. Because of its rare fur pattern mutation it was not often seen. Its yellowish fur had dark blotches and dark stripes on the back; in general it looked darker than the common cheetah. Hunted for its magnificent coat, the king cheetah was among the species threatened with extinction. Owing to the breeding program at the centre, this is no longer the case.

A black honey badger was pacing up and down his enclosure. He seemed to be grumpy and bored, not having a good day by the looks of it. Fittingly, he was dressed in black with a grey mantle covering the top of his head and the back. Had he known that his species was recognised as one of the most fearless creatures, perhaps he would not have taken such a dismal view of life. No one had told him, I guess.

Also called ratel, the honey badger is a creature of dry open grassland and forest. Favourite foods are bulbs and roots and such delicacies as scorpions and snakes and, yes, honey. Not considered an endangered species, it is still under protection in the Krugerpark and the Cape province. However, without a dense population and a slow reproduction rate it was on the list of threatened wildlife.

Among the vulnerable species was the rare brown hyena, a resident of the dry savannah and the semi-desert. Its coat of long rough hair was dark and heavy with a kind of mane on neck and shoulders. The bulky head had large ears with pointed tips, its back was sloping towards the rear. The powerful shoulders and sturdy forelegs were in contrast to shorter and slighter hindquarters. A nocturnal and secretive scavenger, his teeth were specialised in crushing even the strongest bones. The inquisitive curiosity of the animals is described by two researchers, who shared their work, and at times their tent in the desert, with hyenas and other residents. Mark and Delia Owens tell the story in *Cry of the Kalahari.*

We came to a large enclosure where the wild dogs were kept. Irregularly shaped blotches of colours such as black, white, and a pale yellow-brown ensured they were perfectly camouflaged when out hunting. Wagging their white-tipped tails incessantly, the pack greeted us with high-pitched twittering cries. The excitement was not about our presence at all. The eagerly awaited food, which was just being put into their feeding bowls, delighted the dogs. They all dived into their breakfast with relish.

The lean and muscular animals looked almost like domestic dogs, but their large round ears suggested they were not. Those ears enable them to catch far away sounds, which is where they would point their noses to and run, coordinating the hunt on the way. Their high-endurance chasing tactics of tiring out their prey, makes those dogs one of the most efficient hunters.

Close-by, in a separate enclosure, a wild dog mother was taking care of her three pups. They were only a few days old, tiny, sweet and clumsy. She was proudly fussing over them.

Most of the animals in the sanctuary were on the most recent South African Red Data List of 2016; not all were classified as 'threatened, endangered or vulnerable', at least some of them were considered as 'of least concern'.

The de Wildt rescue centre has saved many animal lives, and the staff devote all their efforts to prevent more of the endangered creatures going extinct by the doings of man.

After the tour, I was in need of a bathroom and looked for information. I spotted a colourful wooden board attached to a tree that made me smile. A cheetah pointed the way. With a wry grin on his face, he knew where to go. His footprints on the white arrow below led the way. He, however, was more in a hurry than I was. In the posture of a runner, the figure kept his shoulders back and his torso upright with arms held up so as to give more speed. The facial expression indicated that it was a matter of urgency.

'You definitely left it a bit late, I do hope you made it in time.'

I followed at a slower pace. What a delightful idea to put up such a lovely signpost.

The botanists' discoveries

While the morning was devoted to animals, the afternoon was to plants.

William drove us out to Brummeria, one of Pretoria's suburbs, where we spent the afternoon in the National Botanical Gardens. Established in 1946 and once known as the Transvaal Botanical Gardens, they were opened to the public in 1984.

The gardens featured the varied flora of Africa. The park was beautiful with a waterfall, ponds, lawns, stone bridges, flowers, shrubs, trees. Sections were dedicated to particular ecosystems with their special plants like the succulent garden or the aquatic garden as well as wetlands, woodlands and grasslands.

Plants with a famous relative

Peter was fascinated by the cycads, palm and fern-like plants with dark green feathery leaves. They were of various sizes and diameters. Hardy plants, their natural habitat varies from arid conditions to rain forest areas. Once found on all continents, today some species are endangered and threatened by extinction. Ancient plants, they are slow growing and long-lived, and they can reach a height of several metres. The Brummeria cycads, however, were not the first of the kind we have seen.

One of the tallest and oldest cycads on the planet is living in Kew Royal Botanic Gardens in Richmond in southwest London. Standing more than 4m tall, it can be viewed either from the ground or, climbing up a spiral staircase, by walking on the footbridge. We had seen Kew's large collection in the conservatories on several occasions and admired the celebrated specimen in the Palm House. I remember watching on British television the difficult re-potting operation of the cycad in summer 2009. That delicate and difficult undertaking involved nine gardeners and a crane and took many hours to complete.

The very plant, in 1775, was sent to Kew from South Africa by Francis Masson, one of the garden's plant collectors, sent out to South Africa tasked with collecting seeds and live specimens of native plants and shipping them to London. He came to Cape Town in October 1772 with Captain James Cook's fleet on his second voyage of exploration. At times accompanied by the Swedish botanist and naturalist Dr Carl Peter Thunberg, he travelled around the country on three expeditions hunting for new plants and finding many.

During his second journey in December 1773, Francis Masson made exciting discoveries on the lands of Jacob Kock, a wealthy Boer farmer: "We found here a new palm, of the pith of which the Dutchman told us the Hotten-tots make bread." He described his find: "We observed two species, one about a foot and a half diameter in the stem, and about twelve feet high, with entire leaves; they appeared to be very old, and seldom bore fruit." They looked different: "The other sort had no stem, with the leaves a little ferrated, and lying flat on the ground, which produced a large conical fructification about eighteen inches long, and a foot or more in circumference."[2] Together with many more plants collected, these specimen arrived in Britain, one of which grew into the world-renowned tree.

What historic importance, if any, the cycad in Pretoria's botanical garden had, we did not find out.

In the shade of graceful trees

We sauntered along an avenue of large Bolusanthus or wisteria trees, planted back in 1946. Now grown into mature specimens, they offered much needed shade. Called vanwykshout in Afrikaans, the trees can be found in wooded grasslands around southern Africa. The spectacular tree can get very old, its mauve-coloured flowers drooping from small branches. The species was named after Harry Bolus, businessman, botanist and member of the Linnean Society,

---

[2] An account of three journeys from the Cape Town into the southern parts of Africa, Philosophical Transactions, p292. For more explorer-botanists see Gribbin's *Flower Hunters*.

who organised several plant collecting expeditions around South Africa between 1883 and 1906.

Near the old entrance gate stood the most striking plant in the park, a medium-sized Acacia Sieberiana, named after the 19th century naturalist Franz Wilhelm Sieber from Prague. Its peeling bark gave it the commonly used name of paperbark thorn, or papierbasdoring in Afrikaans. A drought-tolerant and fast growing tree, it can be found in many parts of Africa. Giraffes eat its leaves and twigs, but they were not allowed into the gardens. This specimen, planted in 1947, had grown into a majestic tree. Sitting on top of its many strong branches, its spreading crown was almost as flat as a plate. I found this tree most wonderful. Unfortunately, the imposing tree is not there anymore.

We enjoyed walking around the well maintained sections of the garden, listening to the tunes of the birds, watching the sun moving almost imperceptibly, and the shadows growing distinctly longer. After a three-hour visit, we were picked up where we had been set down.

Thus introduced to some of the animals and plants of South Africa, we felt prepared for our trip to the wild.

Kruger National Park for beginners

Next day, well stocked with bottled drinks and a huge amount of spicy boerewors and biltong, a dried meat jerky, we set off in the afternoon in William's comfortable car. For a while we travelled east on the N4 through vast sweeps of gently rolling landscape. Billowing grasses and wide horizons gave a feeling of endless space and utter emptiness.

The motorway was not very busy, in terms of cars that is. In terms of humans, it was though. Many locals were walking on its shoulder, alone or in pairs or in groups, in single file or next to each other. What was most disturbing was the fact that they crossed through the traffic to get to the other side. They did not even accelerate to reach the opposite shore as fast as possible. Were the scene not a mere 1.5m from the fast moving cars, it could be taken for a stroll in the park. Fortunately, we did not witness any accidents.

At some point we left the main road to continue on minor roads running through green hilly lands. A group of baboons had gathered on a patch of grass close to the road. They looked like idle spectators on a grandstand, watching the few cars that passed through their territory. One of them was bigger than the others and of an imposing appearance. He was probably the dominant male and their leader. He reminded me of Anton Quintana's *Baboon King*, the fierce fighter who, after challenging him, dies at the hands of a reluctant Kikuyu hunter who, expelled by his own human tribe, in turn is accepted by the troop of primates as their new king. We had not seen their kind before in their natural habitat, the baboons at this country road were our first glimpse of the true wild.

After a 400km drive we arrived in Graskop on the Eastern Transvaal Escarpment, a former gold-rush town, now a tourist destination. At the Graskop Hotel we were welcomed by sunbirds greeting us in the garden. The hotel was a very nice and inviting place, and we would have loved to stay longer than just one night, a brief one at that.

On an evening walk around the village we discovered a coffee shop selling Schwarzwälder Kirschtorte. This was not surprising since many people of German descent were living in the region. With heroic willpower, we resisted the lure of such a temptation.

Traffic in the dark

After a short night's sleep in very comfortable beds, we reluctantly got up at the unsociable hour of 4am. With the help of a few cups of strong tea, we slowly collected our senses. Gradually getting into operational gear, we anticipated the day's sightings of lions and leopards. When we left the hotel, the morning was still pitch black.

At this early hour, many locals were already walking along the road, riding their bicycles, or waiting for their bus to go to work. Via the small farming town of Hazyview, we arrived at the border of Krugerpark well before it opened to visitors at 6am. Waiting at the Paul Kruger Gate, we watched the armed guards allowing workers, maintenance vehicles and staff to pass through. At last, we were waved in.

In the reception building right after the gate a form had to be completed, the entrance fee paid and the advice of the ranger to be listened to. The most important was never to get out of the car except at designated spots which were pointed out on a map given to us. Since the park was a malaria area, visitors were urged to take precautions against the disease. Before leaving Britain, we had already started to take the required drugs. Supplied with information and instructions, we were sent on.

Now, we were in the famous park, and the adventure was to begin.

Initiation into wildlife spotting

Kruger National Park, named after Paul Kruger, in 1898 was proclaimed a national park and opened to the public in 1927. From 1902 until retiring in 1945, Major James Stevenson-Hamilton as the principal warden played a decisive role in creating the park. His adventures and tribulations described in his book *South African Eden* illustrate the difficulties and obstacles that presented themselves at the beginning.

Stretching along the border with Mozambique, Kruger lies between the Crocodile River in the south and the Limpopo River in the north. Covering around 20,000sqkm, it is about 350km long and around 65km wide. There are over 4,000km of roads, 13 main camps and 9 entrance gates. A network of tarred and gravelled roads covers the large park.

Entering the park, we expected to catch sight of the famed animals right away. Shortly after the gate and hence still close to the boundaries of the park, we complained to William that he was driving too fast for us to see them.

'Are we not going too fast, how are we supposed to spot them?'

'I am not driving too fast, in fact I am crawling along. You just need to be patient. You will see them sooner or later.'

'But how? I don't see any animal at all! Where is everyone?'

'They are everywhere, you are just not used to discovering them. Just wait a little. We are not even 3km into the park! Don't worry. You will see them, I promise.'

'Hm', allowing a note of slight impatience to enter my voice.

Actually, William was driving even slower than the speed limit. He, of course, knew better and lectured us accordingly. The animals were not to be found so near to the border with a lot of traffic coming and going, and, anyway, we would not see any by expectantly gazing into the grass. But this wise attitude was too much to ask of two novices. On our first moments in the park we just had to see them all immediately. We soon learned otherwise with our own growing experience; gradually developing the right spirit and exercising some patience, we felt to have turned into seasoned wildlife spotters, of sorts at least. We were often driving for a long time without spotting one single creature only to find a cheetah strolling along the road or a herd of elephants materializing from nowhere; surprises and rewards that confirmed our friend's advice.

And indeed not long after William's little speech, we came across a large gathering of gazelles not far from the road. We were delighted. A few minutes on, we discovered a pride of lions slowly moving through the undergrowth in the far distance. We were elated. Later while still impatiently scanning the grass, shrubs and dents, to our relief and excitement, a single elephant was wandering in a green river valley. We were thrilled.

'Told you', came from the right-hand front seat.

These sightings proved William's point and we did not complain any longer. From now on we sat quietly and gazed happily through the windows.

Giraffes fraternizing with zebras and with us

Satara was a large camp situated in open grassland. Before this place was integrated into Krugerpark it was called Wanetzi, where one of Stevenson-Hamilton's rangers was based. At that time, it was an isolated spot: "It was fifty-five miles from the nearest point on the new Selati Railway at Sabi Bridge, with no connecting road or track [...] it was one of the loneliest houses in South Africa – a tiny speck in the wilderness."[3] Today it is easily accessible, offers plenty of accommodation and welcomes thousands of visitors.

We were booked in for two nights. The rondavel for the three of us had one room with three beds and a cupboard as well as a bathroom with a shower. Outside, there were a fridge and a shelf to store food. Neither these nor the rondavel could be locked. We moved in and soon left again to continue our search for wildlife.

We discovered several groups of giraffes and zebras. Since zebras were in the habit of roaming together with giraffes and other grazers for safety, we often saw them not far from each other.

Some of the zebras stayed close together, while others formed wide-spread gatherings. Whether they were all in one large herd, or the get-together consisted of sub-herds or family groups, we were unable to distinguish. Some were grooming each other, while others could be heard whinnying, others were just standing there. But most of the time, the animals were moving around, grazing and keeping in touch with other members of the congregation.

The zebras were Plains or Burchell's zebras. On his journey into the interior of southern Africa in 1811, the explorer and naturalist William John Burchell described them in this way: "The Zebra [...] the stripes [...] being brown

---

[3]South African Eden, p133.

and white, and the brown stripe being double; that is, having a paler stripe within it." He marvelled at their beauty and elegance: "They were the most beautifully marked animals I have ever seen: their clean sleek limbs glittered in the sun, and the brightness and regularity of their striped coat, presented a picture of extraordinary beauty, in which probably they are not surpassed by any quadruped with which we are at present acquainted."[4] Watching the creatures from a short distance, we agreed with Burchell's admiration of these attractive animals.

Their dainty foals were ever so cute and pretty. The toy zebra I used to have as a child would have lost out to their gracefulness and loveliness. But then, they would certainly not appreciate being thrown around, sat on and cuddled all the time.

There were giraffes walking about on their own and also some that preferred the proximity of their mates. A nearby group peered down at us from their lofty height with amiable arrogance. Standing up to 6m tall, they were browsing in the acacia trees and tearing off twigs and leaves. Thoughtfully chewing, they seemed to contemplate us. But one of them got an idea into his head.

Surprisingly, overcome by curiosity, he came closer to see what we were up to. Not more than four metres from the car, he paused and mused and stared. We boldly took this as an invitation for a little chat.

'Hello, how are you doing today?'

'Thank you, I am fine. My friends over there are not interested in anything but eating. How prosaic.'

---

[4]Travels in the interior of Southern Africa, I, p139; II, p315. Like Francis Masson before him, he sent a large collection of plants back to Britain which was later transferred to Kew Gardens; his zoological collection was given to the Oxford University Museum.

'Well, you have to fill your stomach, haven't you.'

'Yes, but talking to visitors like you is so much more interesting and an entertaining change to the daily procedures, I think. The acacia leaves are not going away, but you will in a few moments.'

'What you consider a routine, for us is most exciting, you see. Not often do we meet up with someone who is so much taller and eats nothing but green stuff.'

'Yes, I can imagine. But will you please excuse me, I better go back to my mates lest they disappear and I have to run after them. It was a pleasure speaking with you. You may take a photo if you like.'

'Thank you, that is very kind of you, we will. It was lovely talking to you. All the best to you and your friends.'

Graciously, he allowed us to take a picture. Leaving us, he acknowledged our encounter by nodding and blinking his intelligent eyes with a flutter of his lashes. Ending the brief exchange of civilities, he turned back to his group and the business of eating. From there he looked back at us, his endless neck high in the sky. We waved at him, when driving on.

He sent a faint smile after us.

Threats from the skies

We came across two elephant bulls walking on the grass parallel to the dirt road at a safe distance. It did not escape us that they did not move in a leisurely manner. Watching them for a few minutes, we realized that they were not relaxed at all but appeared to be in a somewhat uneasy mood. Considering their likely tense state of mind, they were not far away enough. We became alert. The car's creeping speed was increased slightly. And sure enough, accelerating their pace noticeably, the elephants were now hurrying along, looking highly concerned. That could become dangerous for us. Something was seriously frightening them. A glance through the rear window revealed the reason for their anxiety.

Seated in the back, I turned and saw a jet black sheet but not much sky.

'Look into your side-mirror, or rather don't', I called out to William at the steering wheel.

'The sky is totally black behind us', he gasped with a troubled frown. 'That does not look too good.'

'Not only for them, it would appear', remarked Peter. 'We better get cracking.'

Unnoticed by us, a charcoal coloured massive wall of menacing clouds had been building up in the far distance behind the animals and the vehicle and was rolling towards our area. Thunder and lightning, not heard or seen by us inside the purring car with the windows closed but by the elephants with a more acute hearing than humans, heralded a mighty storm. It began to darken very quickly with strong gusts of wind developing. Feeling threatened by the danger brewing in their rear, they were visibly getting more and more nervous and agitated.

Both were now panic-stricken.

Abruptly changing their direction and breaking into a kind of run, the elephants suddenly headed towards the road and thus the car. They were huge, and we became seriously alarmed. Their fear combined with their immense size and power posed a real danger to us. The distance between them and us diminished rapidly. We had to get away instantly. So William's foot came down on the accelerator, and, steadily gaining speed, put as much distance between us and them as quickly as he could without giving them another fright.

From a safe distance we saw them cross the road where we had been just a few minutes ago. Both were now in a great rush to get away from the frightening weather front and hastened into a nearby woodland area for shelter, disregarding us completely. We took a deep breath. Seeing their great discomfort, we were hoping they would find the right place to take refuge from the storm and quieten down again.

That was more excitement than we had bargained for. With some urgency and a sigh of relief we too got away from the dark sky as fast as we could.

In the nick of time we reached the camp gate at the closing time of 6pm. Again we had an Afrikaaner dinner, made with the ingredients bought in Pretoria. William prepared the braai on the grill, under his supervision I got the papp ready at the cooking facilities; it fell to Peter to do the dishes later on.

During the night, lions could be heard roaring frequently. The wilderness was just outside the perimeter.

Wildebeest and other beasts

Next morning shortly after the gate had opened we were on our way again. After quite a while of not seeing any animals at all and getting rather frustrated, we found a sizeable troop of baboons near a waterhole. We decided to stay with them for a few moments, it did not bother them in the least. With the engine switched off we watched their noisy antics.

A lot of commotion was going on amid plenty of screaming and heckling. Being of a communicative disposition, most of the gang participated in the general loquaciousness. Some were chasing each other in a tall tree and in nearby bushes. Some preferred the road to the branches and spread out right in front of our car on the warm tarmac. Others approached the vehicle thoroughly inspecting the bonnet, the roof and the tyres. They seemed to be bent on buying the car. Tempting as it was to open the window and discuss a price, we knew that could be dangerous and refrained from doing so. Others were not interested in the object on wheels and could not care less. After some time, all of them got bored and slowly moved to another place. And so did we.

Soon, a large gathering of wildebeest and zebras came into view not far from the road. Besides with giraffe, zebras associate also with the large antelopes. While the zebras were busily grazing and keeping watch, many of the wildebeest were happily resting on the ground. One of the missionaries who travelled in southern Africa in the middle of 19th century described the animal thus: "Of all animals of South Africa the gnu has the most extraordinary form: it has the eyes, nostrils, and colour of the buffalo, the feet of antelope, the mane and body of the ass, the neck and shoulders of the horse, which it resembles also in its movements."[5] In Bavaria in southern Germany, a creature made up of many unmatching parts answering the description by the man of the cloth, would be called a Wolperdinger, a mythological creature of the European Alps. The wildebeest would probably mind a comparison.

A family of warthogs stared at us uneasily from their cover under a cluster of bushes. The mother looked at the car and was not happy about its presence. Considering the situation for a while, she gathered her flock of children, and they all retreated into the dense clump of shrubs wishing not to be seen. Respecting their preference for privacy, we moved away.

On a piece of open land, we came across a lonely buffalo just standing there in the grass. Not making even the smallest movement, black and big, he looked like a statue. Was he dozing and dreaming, or just immersed in reflections of his own, I wondered. He was as massive as his large horns were impressive. Those over our gate back at my childhood home once had adorned a beast as majestic as this one.

I thought about telling him about my horns but felt that might be insensitive and hurt his feelings. To make up for my inappropiate idea, I instead told him that he was a splendid and majestic creature. My compliment was accepted with nonchalance. Being conscious of his awe-inspiring magnificence himself, he did not even blink.

A flummoxed rhino

The grasslands we passed next were dotted with tall green bushes offering shade and welcome cover. A wonderful area to drive through. But no creatures anywhere near; or so we thought.

---

[5]Eugène Casalis, The Basutos or twenty-three years in South Africa, p32.

All of a sudden, a white or square-lipped rhino broke through the dense shrubs on our right and came to a halt just two metres in front of the car. We had not seen or heard anything, and evidently he had not either. Generally, rhinos have keen hearing and quite a good sense of smell, but they do not have good vision. This fellow was not seeing very well and may be not hearing terribly well either, because his thoughts were absorbed with more important topics than crossing a country lane in safety.

Now faced with reality, he was perplexed. In bewilderment, he stomped back and forth looking puzzled and mystified. He might also be irritated by something, perhaps he was troubled by the fuel emissions or by something else we were not aware of. Raking his brains, he tried to identify that smell or the shiny object or whatever it was that upset him. He eyed the car, but did not move. He was just standing there, thinking things over and reflecting.

After a few more minutes of deliberating and head-scratching, the rhino arrived at a temporary resolve and briskly trotted across the gravel road right in front of the car without one more glance in our direction. He again came to a halt in the long grass, looked back at the road, hesitated again, and concluded the mental process of coming to a final decision. He collected his thoughts for good and vanished into the bushes.

Then we found another buffalo, again without a herd anywhere in the vicinity. Like the first one, he was not moving but stood still in the middle of a dust pan. Having an appointment with the hygiene specialists, he was being worked on by a flock of red-billed oxpeckers. The small cleaner birds were looking for parasites in the nostrils and the ears as well as on the skin and in the coat of the huge animal. The enormous beast indulged in being pampered and therefore did not give us one look. The most dangerous animal of Africa looked like a well cared-for and most valued customer in a bush beauty salon.

Warfare in the grass

On a stretch of savannah we were about to witness that size is not everything. About 10m from the car we noticed two exceptionally tall birds.

Standing about 1.30m tall, they were clad in grey-cream attire with black wing-tips and a yellow patch on the cheeks. Black half-length trousers and a long tail-bar added to their grandeur. They were secretary birds, looking like stern officials of times past, conscious of their role and task. The acclaimed researcher and film-maker Laurens van der Post described them beautifully: "Of all the creatures, none dressed as well as the birds of Africa. [...] Even the soberest ones among them, which went about the country austere as elders of the Dutch Reformed Church collecting from parsimonious congregations on Sunday mornings – the old-fashioned storks in black and white, or the secretary-birds with their stiff starched fronts and frock coats – their dress was always of an impeccable taste."[6] Long-legged and graceful, they had an air of stateliness and high rank about them.

We watched the pair striding on the open grass land with great dignity and a thoughtful nod. Quite inoffensively and casually it seemed to us. But not to other creatures. They did not just happen to perambulate right here. In fact, far from caring for the souls of their flock, they were on a different mission altogether: they were birds-of-prey. Intentionally or accidentally, the two secretaries were walking right into a nesting area on the ground which we could not see.

Rising from the grass all of a sudden, a large flock of small birds launched a vigorous defence of their eggs or chicks. Like arrow-headed torpedoes, all the tiny birds were staging a perfectly coordinated attack on the giant assailants. Surprised and irritated, the secretaries tried to fend off the massive onslaught by spreading their large wings. Their attempt of intimidating and threatening the feathered army failed miserably though. Their display of size did not impress the little birds at all. Relentlessly and incessantly they kept on defending their brood. The small and agile combatants were just too numerous. In the end, outnumbered and overwhelmed, the tall secretaries had to retreat and take refuge in the sky. The triumphant birds settled down once more to their parenting duties.

We applauded the small birds' bravery, determination, and utter fearlessness in the face of serious danger.

Taking to the air in a clumsy way, the large birds were clearly more at home on the ground. Having adopted ter-

---

[6] Heart of the hunter, p95-96.

restrial hunting habits, secretary birds were in fact perfectly adapted for long-distance treks through semi-arid open grassland on their search for a meal. Skilled hunters, they preyed on snakes, larger insects in particular locusts, small mammals and young birds and eggs. Their numbers were said to be decreasing through invasions of pastoralists and cultivators. We were lucky enough to spot the dramatic birds on more than one occasion.

On the bank of a small river we watched two magnificent kingfishers at work. In their colourful plumage of royal blue to malachite, intense orange, and white patches they could not be missed. Perched on branches they were following any movement in the water, ready to dive down and retrieve their reward. We discovered a few eagles checking their territory. Further down, a few inconspicuous looking crocodiles were lurking in the muddy water, slowly gliding along. Nearby, two elegant goliath herons were also on the lookout for a meal. The water level here was rather low, giving both of them plenty of easy opportunities to find what they were hoping for.

Yawns and bellows

Our noontime destination was the strikingly located Olifants Camp, our most northern point in the Kruger. Opened in 1960, it had rondavels, bungalows and a restaurant. The camp appeared to be a comfortable and inviting place and looked well kept with wonderful trees, plenty of space and a nice lawn area. The few housekeeping maids to be seen were dressed in crisp green uniforms, finishing their duties for the day. No house guests could be seen, we were the only visitors. At this time of day it was hot and very quiet.

Having done all the driving for several hours, William was taking a well deserved nap on one of the benches under the trees. Peter and I were far too excited to succumb to $33°C/91.4°F$, in the shade. Under normal circumstances I would hardly be able to function in the heat, but the location of the camp had too much to offer. We went in search for a suitable place for sighting animals and found the perfect vantage point for watching hippos.

Sitting high up on a ridge above Olifants River, the camp commanded wide views over the gently rolling land and the river just below. The bench we chose, as a perch and for lunch, was located at a spectacular lookout right on top of the cliffs high above the water. With boerewors in one hand and binoculars in the other, we scanned the near and far for animals. Not much was going on because at this time of day, by then almost 2pm, the temperature was at its peak.

Therefore most animals were resting in the shade under bushes and trees. On the hill opposite the camp, we discovered a few zebras and wildebeest dozing away in the heat. Except for the occasional ear flapping or eye blinking, there was no movement to be seen.

In the river below, however, no rest was required. A pod of hippos frolicked in their wet and cool home. They splashed noisily, grunting and bellowing. Some were submerged with only their head visible. The small eyes and little ears were constantly scanning their surroundings. Others were lazing beneath the surface, emerging every few minutes to draw breath and check on their mates. One was yawning to the nearest neighbour, a threat display to keep his personal space.

Blowing bubbles, one of the biggest hippos was just sinking into the depth with a despondent look on his large face. I thought that might be Mvu, resigning himself to his accepting the dinner invitation of Kamba, the tortoise, and his scheming wife, who together had tricked him into thinking that the little tortoise was just as strong as the massive haughty hippo and Njobvu, the angry powerful elephant. Having duped them into a tug-of-war, the deluded tortoise regarded himself on an equal footing with the giants and was very proud of his new standing. According to the old African tale of *Tortoise Triumphant* it is more essential to have brains than to be possessed of strength and bulk.

A mother and her calf wandered off to a near sandbank trampling down the green grass with their huge feet, squashing every blade there was. The youngster stayed close behind her for protection. I did not think anyone would be foolish enough to charge with such a colossal mother as opponent; even crocodiles are wise enough not to attempt it.

The camp offered a truly fantastic spot to gaze across the land which could hardly be surpassed. Yet, in a way it was matched by another one six months later, on top of the Great Wall of China. Instead of a noisy hippo congregation for entertainment, there were the relentless vendors besieging us and praising their wares. On that occasion, I wished I was back on the Olifants cliff.

We stayed on our bench for quite some time. On the slope across the river, all creatures continued relaxing out of the sun. Happily sitting and watching, we waited for William to finish his siesta. He joined us to observe the big animals at our feet. They did their best to entertain him with bickering and posturing.

On our way back, on a stretch of open land, a light-brown cat with dark spots threaded its way through the tall grass towards a group of trees. No doubt, it was Kipling's leopard Spots of the *Just So Stories* who swiftly moved up to 'a leafy branch' and looked 'like sunshine sifting through the leaves'. From his perch he stared at us, wishing not to be disturbed. We understood and left for Satara.

Childhood games

It was our day of departure. The day's itinerary led us to the southern section of the Kruger, leaving the park at Malelane via Tshokwane and Lower Sabie and continuing to the old gold-rush area for a very brief tour. But before we got there, we had more than one exciting encounter.

At Tshokwane the trees were buzzing with hundreds of small birds. Before it was made into the modern picnic site, it had been one of Major Stevenson-Hamilton's stops on his tours around the Sabi Reserve he was in charge of. "It provided excellent grazing and water; was a good central point for minor expeditions, [...] and held more game and lions to the square mile than any other part of the Reserve."[7] Except for the birds no animals were to be seen. At his time, there had been a few kraals in the area, the chief of which had been called Tshokwane.

On a slope not very far from the road, a group of about eighteen elephants was strung out among low green bushes and brown long grass. They slowly moved down, obviously intending to go to some place on the opposite side of the road. They were in no hurry, enjoying the day. Keeping our distance, we settled down to watch them for a while.

It was a family of all sizes and ages. Some of them, having shiny backs, had just been wallowing somewhere in the mud. Their young were running around wherever their fancy took them but were reined in by sharp glances. Like any kids of any species, the youngsters were investigating the shrubs and whatever appeared worth exploring, or they were playing hide and seek with their willing cousins. They were supervised by their mothers, aunts or older sisters, trunks short and long constantly sniffing, assessing, touching and re-assuring. The adults took a more relaxed view

---

[7]South African Eden, p145-146.

on matters, nonetheless watching with attention the intentions and whereabouts of their charges. Having satisfied their desire for a nibble and a game, the calves were summoned, and the herd began moving in our direction.

They walked towards the road with their youngsters kept close between them. They did not seem at all disturbed or upset by our presence, sensing our harmlessness. In measured steps without any haste, the herd slowly crossed the road about 10m from the car, not minding us at all.

Fascinated and awed, we sat and watched.

Hippos in disguise

Taking the Lower Sabie and the Gomondwane Road we came to Hippo Pool close to Crocodile Bridge Gate near the south eastern corner of the Krugerpark. Here a large community of hippos had made their home in a sheltered bend of the Crocodile River. When we arrived, an armed field ranger was just dismounting his bicycle to inspect one more checkpoint on his patrol. He motioned us to get out of the car and join him. Delighted by this unexpected invitation, we did not hesitate.

We followed him over a wooden bridge to the river onto a boardwalk through the reeds. It was remarkably quiet without a sound emanating from anywhere, no grunts or bellows coming from the water. No hippo was to be seen or heard, neither in the pond nor anywhere else, it was just vegetation and water. Considering that there were said to be many of them, where were they?

But the place had not been named for nothing.

The ranger, of course, knew their habits and their prefered spots. He knew where they were, particularly one of them. He banged two small stones together, and, to our utter surprise, out of the dense reeds almost right next to our feet a large hippo heaved himself up and plunged back into the water with an almighty splash. The water spilled over the boardwalk and drenched our shoes.

Despite his bulk, he had been disguised by the greenery, perfectly succeeding in concealing himself. Covered by the green tall thin stems of the grass, he had observed us, quietly waiting and watching from his hiding place. We had not even noticed him, close that he was.

The ranger smiled.

From the safety of the water the hippo was now eyeing us with curiosity, while all his mates conspired to remain well hidden. Though the area was inhabited by dozens of them, the huge animals managed to make themselves entirely invisible.

The hippos chuckled.

We greatly admired their ability and strategy of not being there.

Lionesses at my window

Out in the wild country, you never know what might come up.

Continuing our route via the Crocodile River Road, we headed towards Malelane through what was the former Sabi Game Reserve prior to becoming part of Kruger National Park.

We were in a wooded and hilly area with dense vegetation, interspersed with sections of open grassland. Coming round a bend of the road the three of us were startled. We stiffened in surprise and some degree of fright. The car came to a sudden but carefully balanced halt.

Again, William's lecture proved right. When you are looking for the animals, you won't find them. You will see them, when you are not searching. They will just show up in front of you, which is exactly what happened.

Two lionesses ambled towards us at a leisurely pace, striding right in front of a crawling pickup and a car behind. No doubt, they had heard or smelled or sensed our vehicle move on the crunching gravel road long before we came into view.

While two of Africa's successful hunters were approaching the car, we became slightly worried as they walked straight towards it. Lions almost marching into you is positively unnerving.

'They are aiming for the car!'

'Why should they, doesn't taste nice. Would you wish to eat the cables or the metal frame?'

'All nonsense! I wouldn't want to eat us either. It is not us they are after, they are not stupid.'

They could easily have jumped onto the vehicle to have a better view of the area, using it as a high seat just like human hunters. But they had no such intentions.

While the lionesses kept walking in the middle of the road, the car slowly and gently reversed to one side of the road, giving them more room to pass. Keeping a good distance to them made us a little less uneasy. That feeling did not last for more than a second though.

They got much closer. They chose to move right along the vehicle passing the windows at no distance at all, their coat almost brushing the doors. Transfixed, we sat perfectly still, not turning our heads, not looking into their faces. My heart leaped and my pulse took off, but the two lionesses just ignored us entirely.

Their pricked ears meant serious business, the hunters had something more interesting on their minds. They had noticed a group of wary impala not far away, for whom their attention was abating though while approaching. Behind our car they stopped in the middle of the road, staring intently and listening motionlessly up the slope left of the road. Their postures changed from that of an idle and bored stroller into that of a keen and alert predator. The lionesses must have spotted more rewarding prey, they disappeared swiftly into the shrubs. We could not see them any longer or discover what they were after. With the mortal danger gone away for the moment at least, the impala relaxed and returned their attention to eating.

Like the antelope, we also calmed down after that spine-tingling experience.

Too many lions at first

Before the Sabi Reserve became part of the Krugerpark, lions had been given an unpleasant time. As most herbivores had been killed in huge numbers by native and white hunters, the amount of carnivores was too plentiful in proportion. One of the jobs of the early rangers had been establishing the right balance between extinction and over-population, resulting in the destruction of almost all the lions that roamed the large district.

One of the rangers tasked with reducing their numbers was Harold Trollope, a respected hunter renowned for his first-rate marksmanship and intimate knowledge of the veld. Bushwise and armed with his trusted rifle he moved stealthily, cautiously and noiselessly. Familiar with the wild from boyhood, he was able to distinguish the animals by the faintest sounds that reached his ears. Hunting with a well-trained horse and his efficient dogs, he almost never missed his target.

Sergeant Harry Wolhuter, a hunter and, before taking on the job in the game reserve, a member of Steinacker's Horse, a volunteer corps in the Boer War, was also engaged in bringing down the number of lions. This done, he avoided having to kill any more lions, but was forced once when he and his horse were attacked by two lions at night. In his new life, he instead took care of the animals' well-being and enjoyed the transformation: "I was now on the eve of a completely new experience; for henceforth I was to protect game, instead of hunting it." Changing sides gave him a new perspective on wildlife: "My long, subsequent experience has taught me that, thrilling though the pleasures of shooting undoubtedly are, infinitely greater and more lasting pleasure and interest can be obtained from the observation and study of wild animals, unafraid and uninterfered with, in their natural haunts; and I have never regretted my metamorphosis from hunter to guardian!"[8] He observed lions and their behaviour on many occasions, which he narrates in detail in his reminiscences about forty-four years as a game ranger.

We left Kruger National Park through Malelane Gate. Instead of returning straight to Pretoria, we took a detour through what was once the land of swarms of hopeful prospectors.

Through gold-rush country

In the 19th century, gold was discovered in the Transvaal, part of which is now called Mpumalanga. The former gold mining area was not very far from Malelane. From Nelspruit we took the road to Sabie, making a little roundtrip through what were once the fields of many diggers' golden optimism and then down to the N4 back to Pretoria.

We travelled through the Mpumalanga Drakensberg region, a section of the Great Escarpment, the chain of mountains stretching from the Eastern Cape to Limpopo Province. High peaks and steep slopes, narrow valleys and deep gullies, as well as large waterfalls were typical. The high mountain range dominated the region, and it once played

---

[8]Memories of a game ranger, p83.

a vital and dramatic role in the food supply of the miners and the newly founded towns.

As I knew about the difficulties of crossing the mountains at that time from one of my favourite books, I was glad we drove through the districts albeit more for a glimpse than a visit.

A few mining towns

First we came to Sabie, a small country town. Not much reminded us of its high-flying time in the 1870s. Today it has turned from gold exploration to tourism and forestry. The place is surrounded by commercial plantations of pine and eucalyptus trees after the indigenous forest had been cut down in the late 19th century for use in the mines and to make firewood for the workers. Today, thanks to a number of afforestation programs the region has one of the largest man-made forests of the world. Around the town, a thriving timber-industry has developed into the 21st century.

In 1874, gold had been found in Pilgrim's Rest, attracting hundreds of fortune hunters. With the decline of gold production most mines were closed around 1913. The main street looked just the same as it had in those times. The very small but charming town is now a National Monument, mainly benefitting from its history and proximity to Kruger National Park.

Lydenburg, now Mashishing, was founded in 1850 by a group of Vortrekkers. It has developed into a substantial town but still with the appeal of a small town. With the discovery of gold in 1873, the place had become a magnet attracting masses of people to the area who hoped to strike it rich.

In the wake of the diggers came labourers, hunters, agents, hawkers, traders, and beasts of burden.

Waggons, stores and business

The evolving towns and the prospectors' camps all needed supplies, from food and liquor to tools and spare-parts. They were dependent on regular deliveries offered by transport-riders, drivers and oxen. It proved to be a most difficult and laborious task and a major operation to satisfy that demand.

The problem of getting equipment, stores, and goods into the interior was solved by drafting in ox-waggons. "So from the Lydenburg Goldfields prospectors 'humping their swags' or driving their small packdonkeys spread afield, and transport-riders with their longspans and rumbling waggons followed." Demand to shift material grew to such an extent that more and more carts had to be made, as *The Farmers Chronicle* announced on November 14, 1889: "We are exceedingly pleased to hear that our energetic townsman Mr. George Patmore has just received an order to manufacture sixty new wagons for the Gold Fields trade." Those carts had to be able to carry very heavy bulky loads and withstand the extreme rigours of the road. The digging boom created income for wheelwrights, blacksmiths and toolmakers as well as for grocers and brewers, and many more.

Using previous tracks, a transport 'road' of sorts had been established between the mining fields and the nearest port, Lourenço Marques in Portuguese East Africa, today's Maputo in Mozambique. The distance between the gold fields and the Indian Ocean, around 300km, was dotted by outspan places, where the exhausted men and over-fatigued oxen could rest for the night. Some had developed into substantial camps with "the tents of lone prospectors, the cabins of the diggers, and the grass wayside shanties of the traders."

One of the men on the supply road between the mines and Delagoa Bay wrote down his adventures in the early 1900s, after he had left "the charm of a life of freedom and complete independence – a life in which a man goes as and where he lists, and carries his home with him" and became a politician and an author. Sir Percy Fitzpatrick, in his wonderful book *Jock of the Bushveld*, described the hardships and pleasures of the waggon route that he had experienced in the company of his bushwise hunting dog Jock in the 1880s.[9]

The challenging days of the transport-riders spring from the pages of the book.

Yells, whips, yokes and grunts

Not the bushveld or the streams that had to be crossed posed the greatest difficulties and complications for the transport crews, it was the horrendously steep walls of the Drakensberg Chain.

The looming mountain range, called the Berg for short, was a major obstacle for the transport riders and their fully loaded bullock-waggons during the gold-mining boom. "The Berg stood up before us like an impassable barrier. Looked at from below, the prospect was despairing – from above, appalling." Seen from either end, the rugged terrain and the sheer gradient of the ascent to the passes or the descent down to the lowveld were deemed near impossible to negotiate. But men and oxen managed to do just that.

It was a struggle to get up or down the precipitous mountain. As a proper road in the true sense did not exist, waggons and animals had to navigate their way between rocks and boulders along the tortuous scarp.

---

[9] Jock of the Bushveld, p14, 15, 17.

The toughness of manoeuvring the waggon-trains up or down the Drakensberg was not for the wimpish. Nerves of steel and an iron will were key qualities. The strenuous efforts and supreme abilities required for getting the supplies to the diggers deserve to be recalled.

The job was so difficult, for both men and animals, that a perfect understanding and mutual trust between them was vital to get up or down that awful mountain. "Heart and training in the cattle, skill and judgement in the driver, are needed there; for the Berg is a searching test of man and beast." Bringing in provisions demanded the utmost of both: "Some, double-spanned and relieved of half their three-ton loads, will stick for a whole day where the pull is steepest, the road too narrow to swing the spans, and the curves too sharp to let the fifteen couples of bewildered and despairing oxen get a straight pull." Adjusting the cargo's weight to the gradient and condition of the road was the only strategy to reach the top.

It was indispensable to know the character of the animals: "Whilst others will pass along slowly but steadily and without check, knowing what each beast will do and stand, when to urge and when to ease it, when and where to stop them for a blow, and how to get them all leaning to the yoke, ready and willing for the 'heave together' that is essential for restarting a heavy load against such a hill."[10]

What a formidable challenge the Drakensberg had been for men and animals. The route through the bushveld, across the rivers and over the high passes was abandoned in

---

[10] Jock of the Bushveld, p223, 224-225. The text is illustrated opposite p226, showing the drama of the route. Also Thomas Baines, F.R.G.S., artist, adventurer and explorer travelled in the 1870s in the area, recording his experiences in numerous sketches. His pencil and water-colour drawing 'Climbing the heights of the Drakensberg' on May 31, 1871 shows such a scene. Wallis, p202.

1892 with the arrival at Nelspruit of the railway line to and from the coast. With faster, cheaper and more convenient transportation now available, and, as soon after, oxen and waggons were commandeered by the armed forces in the Anglo-Boer War, the transport crews became redundant.

Back to the dogs

On the way back to Pretoria we came through the region's dramatic landscape between Krugerpark and the former goldrush towns. The valleys, streams, grassy slopes and the mountain peaks in the distance again evoked Sir Fitzpatrick's reminiscences.

Our route along the R533 gave us an idea of the challenges those riders, drivers and animals had to overcome. Negotiating innumerable bends, the winding road rose to an altitude of about 1800m above sea level. We arrived at Robbers' Pass. Whether the transport crews had ever to deal with an ambush or an attack, I do not recall. In 1897, the passengers on a stage coach were forced at gunpoint to leave their gold and cash to armed highwayman on the very spot.

Verraaiersnek on the road to Lydenburg/Mashishing was another pass, which was only about 1300m and less demanding to get to. For a car with a powerful engine the run was easy, but for oxen and men it surely had been gruelling.

Driving through the mountainous region in a comfortable vehicle of the 21st century, it seemed almost impossible to imagine the pains of the transport crews in the late 19th century. To us, the views over the escarpment were breathtaking and beautiful, for the waggon drivers and their animals they were nothing but repulsive and terrifying.

In the evening we were back at William's house, where it was raining for a change.

The dogs were delighted to have company again. They followed us around and did not leave us out of their sight. I wonder how they would have responded had we told them about our adventure with the lionesses. They probably would have howled. We didn't, and they just wagged their tails pleased we were back.

We did not immediately fly back to Britain. Another excursion of a few days was scheduled to begin the following day. While William temporarily returned to his desk, Peter and I were off to another exercise in exploring more mountain landscapes and new aspects of the African-European past.

'We flattered ourselves that we should one day see the supreme chief of the country take up his abode with us'

Glimpses of Lesotho

Land of the mountains

Next day, Peter and I travelled to Lesotho, the kingdom high in the mountains, which, at almost 3,500m, has the highest peak in southern Africa. Surrounded by the Republic of South Africa, the continent's most industrialized nation, it is one of the least developed countries in the world.

There was a personal reason for our visit. We had not seen Ann since she had taken up a position at the National University of Lesotho. Since it was uncertain for how long she might stay, we decided to pay her a visit as we were almost in the neighbourhood.

We reckoned that air travel from London to Roma takes longer than road travel from Pretoria. As it turned out our optimism was somewhat misplaced.

Disgruntled roosters on the seats

William gave us a lift to Pretoria central bus station. He was to join us in Roma a few days later.

It had been arranged for Ann to pick us up at the scheduled arrival time of 3pm at the bus terminal in Bloemfontein, about 140km from the Lesotho border.

At 8am, on time, the Translux coach departed for the journey via Johannesburg, Parys and Welkom. All three places, as those in the Drakensberg region, were towns that came into being during or in the wake of the gold rush, which had gripped the Witwatersrand from the 1880s onwards. While the first has developed into a metropolis with a population of around six million and a world-wide importance, the two other towns are still only small or medium-sized with Parys under 10,000 and Welkom of about 66,000 inhabitants, both with touristic and commercial ambitions. All are still involved in gold mining.

Not long after Johannesburg and just over one hour into our trip the wiper motor broke down, and the driver decided he could not go any further without a new one. He rang headquarters to arrange for the immediate delivery of a replacement, which, as he was told, should take no longer than one and a half hours. He drove to the nearest service station to find a suitable parking lot. We disembarked and hoped for the best. In the end, it took nearly three hours for the new motor to be sent to the waiting coach. Once a mechanic with the spare parts had arrived and the problem got fixed, the driver and his passengers were happy, and the journey continued.

The coach called at many stops along the route, picking up and setting down passengers with their varied cargo on the way. It was a mixture between a local shuttle and a long-distance connection. The cluckcluck complaints of the chickens added entertainment to the experience. We were the only foreigners on board.

After an interesting drive through industrial areas, agricultural regions and wide sweeps of grassland for grazing, the coach arrived in Bloemfontein at about 7pm instead of 3pm. It took us about eleven hours to cover 485km. It had not rained one drop.

Ann had been waiting for over four hours without managing to get any information at the bus terminal, why the coach was not arriving in time, or when it might be expected. Our attempts to warn her of the delay while waiting for the motor to arrive were unsuccessful as the phones were not working.

After two years in an African environment she had become seasoned and rather philosophical about such trifles.

Worse was yet to come.

Scary moments in a black night

We headed for Lesotho. As it was dark, there was nothing
for us to see but a few lights from villages in the distance.
We knew that we were driving through a region that, like
many others, had a turbulent history. The Caledon Valley
was a fertile area that had been fought over by a variety of
factions at various times. In the 19th century in particular,
it had experienced waves of conflicts.

Boers disenchanted with reforms introduced by British
authorities moved beyond the Orange River boundary, while
British settlers and speculators streamed in from the Eastern Cape looking for land. Owing to several prolonged
droughts, among other reasons, numerous ethnic groups
such as the Ndebele, Zulu, Khoi, Basuto, Nguni, Tswana,
San, Griqua, Xhosa, Rolong wandered around the land in
search of food and new pasture. With so many parties
sweeping through, collisions were inevitable. Traditional
rivalries resurfaced, new ones emerged; raiding, displac-
ing, dispersing and killing followed. Pushing through the
area, the European pioneers and the various African peoples fought over territories and boundaries. Tensions are
still simmering today.

Ann's vehicle had presented her with a few problems,
but she hoped it was now more reliable after several maintenance visits to a garage. Still, she dreaded the worst.

And it did happen. The car broke down.

Place and hour were most unfortunate. It was late,
pitch dark and in a wooded area in the middle of nowhere,
far from any town or settlement. We learned that none
of the passing cars, few as they were, could be expected
to stop for fear of being ambushed, hijacked, kidnapped,
robbed or even killed by hidden gunmen. On the other
hand, people in a broken down vehicle were also at the

same risk of being attacked at gunpoint. Those hostilities of the past in the back of our minds and the still unbalanced situation following apartheid, we were rather nervous about the dangerous situation.

We were stuck in the dead of night without any prospect of assistance. That was extremely worrying.

Since it was not the first time that Ann's car refused to move, she hoped it did not let her down completely on this unlucky occasion. She was deeply concerned, as nothing could be done. Her experience had told her that, after a while, the car might work again. Perhaps. We just had to patiently sit it out and, as in the morning at the service station, hope for the best. Sure enough, after an endless wait the vehicle could be restarted. We heaved a great sigh of relief. Without further problems we continued our trip through the dark.

With two technical mishaps one after another on our way to Lesotho, I wondered what was awaiting us in that unknown country.

More than a bridge

Before crossing the Caledon or Mohokare River at Maseru Bridge into Lesotho, we passed a vast bus station. Late at night it was busy with vehicles and crowded with people: men clad in blankets carrying bags and boxes, women holding on to their luggage, buses preparing for departure, minivans loading up to capacity, and taxis arriving from Maseru.

The Basuto men and women were travelling to their place of work in South Africa, namely to the diamond and gold mines in Kimberley and Witwatersrand and to places in and around Johannesburg and other cities. They were also employed in the construction and service sector. An extensive network of long-distance buses was running regularly from the Lesotho border to provide overnight transport for the cross-border workforce. Migrant labour was a strong tie, linking the economy of Lesotho to that of her neighbour.

Once the granary for the Orange Free State and the Eastern Cape in the 19th century, since the 20th century Lesotho has not been able to feed itself anymore and has become one of the world's poorest countries. The factors that led to the country's shrinking agricultural production were manifold: erosion due to soil being blown and washed away, agrarian land overworked by farming of maize, sorghum and wheat; inadequate livestock management like overstocking and overgrazing; a series of years of drought, lack of adequate tools and traction, and a shortage of able-bodied farm workers.

The availability of arable land decreased not only because of bad soil management but also because of growing human settlement in the lowlands. Increased rural poverty led to export of labour which generated income to sustain families, fields, farms and herds back home. With a high unemployment rate hovering around 25-30% for years and half the population living below the international poverty line, the country of Lesotho is ranking near the bottom of the Human Development Index of the United Nations.

Disco boom at the border post

The Lesotho border control was the most unusual we have ever passed through on our trips abroad. Heavy disco sound came booming out of the building. Frequently travelling between South Africa and Lesotho, this was not unusual to Ann. While Peter and I could not believe our ears, she ushered us in.

Unusual looking characters were greeting us to inspect our travel documents. Instead of wearing uniforms or anything remotely meeting that term, the law enforcement officials were attired in Jeans, T-Shirts and blankets. Their feet in sneakers and the rest of their bodies were moving rhythmically to the beat of the hot music. We had never seen a dancing border post in party mood.

Since Ann was one of the limited number of temporary residents in the country and often moving between both countries, she knew that they knew her. She turned on the charm and with big smiles practiced her interpersonal skills on them. We were impressed by her proficiency in the Sesotho language.

The border post was open twenty-four hours. At the time, close to midnight, we were the only travellers wishing to get into the country. We went through the formalities of immigration. One of the officers took an interest in Peter's passport which was plastered with visas. He inspected every page. Searching for the right one, he was pointing out to himself every letter with his finger, very slowly. Being satisfied with his findings, he returned the document and waved us on with a smile. Amazed and amused, we left the checkpoint to drive on to Roma, another dark 35km.

Ann swung her car into the campus of the National University of Lesotho. We had made it despite various technical issues with the coach and the car. Not quite so. We had to face yet another kind of uncooperation.

The guards at the entrance gate were in an ungenerous mood and not inclined to let us pass. Even though Ann was well known to them, they pretended not to recognize her or her car and insisted on searching the boot for weapons. She was not unused to being subjected to special treatment. While being angry, she knew from experience that it was best to comply. Using her charm and her language skills helped somewhat, and at long last we were given the all clear and whisked through the barrier.

It was past midnight, it had taken us over sixteen hours to get from Pretoria to Roma, probably more than by plane from the UK via Maseru, the country's main airport.

Hair-raising tales

Our first day in Lesotho introduced us to some details about Ann's life and some background about the country and its people.

After a short walk around the campus we ventured outside the gate for a drive up the close-by hills. We did not get far. As Ann had suspected, the capricious car was not able to tackle the steep gravel road. Half way up it refused to climb one inch further. So, we had to accept defeat and turn back. A more powerful engine was needed.

That day, we did not hire a tougher car but went for lunch instead. Mmelesi Lodge was the right place to offset our disappointment with a nice meal and a glass of fine wine.

Which in turn provided the perfect counterpoint for Ann's appalling stories about life in Lesotho.

Desperation and destitution

From the start, she had been pursued by persistent offers from determined locals to do her washing and cleaning. She was of course aware that people in Lesotho were desperate for a job and money and felt a duty to assist them. Understanding that by hiring a domestic help she was supporting a family, she conceded after a while, otherwise there would have been no end to her being besieged. Occasionally, Ann was able to help, with clothes, money, or a lift.

From conversations with local people, in particular with the women, Ann learned about the pressures of the bride-price, the power of the healers, the lack of medical care, the decline of family ties, the constant pregnancies, the high rate of infant mortality, the large number of children, the wives' suffering at the hands of their husbands, the work-load for women, the need to provide for their families, the absence of their men. She knew stories of hunger, malnutrition, illness, alcoholism, murder, rape, jealousy, superstition, lynchings, migrant labour, witch-hunts, harsh winters, bad roads, devastating poverty and wife beatings, and HIV, to name but a few.

Illiteracy, tradition, long practiced backwardness and leadership disputes within the tribal government did nothing to improve the generally dire situation of the families of Lesotho.

No WLAN but bullets

The consequences of general poverty, lack of investment, meagre resources and deficient management of utilities also had an effect on her own existence.

Ann had to cope with regular breakdowns of the communication systems with phones, internet and email not working for days or even weeks. A mobile phone network was not in existence. Often the university could not be reached by phone, reason being that either the lines were out of order, or the operators could not bring themselves to do their job, it was just too bothersome. We had tried for days to get hold of her which proved to be a near futile exercise.

Her spacious flat with balcony and mountain view did have wooden flooring but no heating system of any kind, which was slightly unpleasant in winter at often less than 10°C below zero. Electric fan heaters, when available at all, were not very efficient. Unannounced water rationings and frequent power cuts made life not easy. After dark, women were not supposed to walk around the campus because it was dangerous. The perimeter fence had been cut at several places and left in that state, no one took the trouble to repair it.

Burglaries in the living quarters were by no means unusual, she had uninvited visitors in the dead of night more than once. Theft, vandalism or car break-ins happened almost on a daily basis. Luckily, exposure to weapons and violence in the Staff Club was not a regular event. One evening, however, she was in the bar of the club together with almost a dozen colleagues, when three armed men burst in, fired a shot and forced one of them to open the till at gunpoint. Not finding any serious amount of money, the robbers debated whether to shoot that person or not. In the end they decided against such action, instead grabbed the money and handbags and disappeared into the dark night.

We appreciated Ann's courage, resilience and willingness to keep up with it all. As it turned out, she stuck it out for more than a decade before taking up a job in another country, toughened up quite a bit, I suppose.

The missionaries' zeal

In Morija we paid a brief visit to the local museum and archives. A collection of ethnographic and historical exhibits reflected Lesotho's history, in particular the country's native past and its exploration by Europeans. There were various documents dating back to the beginnings of the settlement, rare books, mission papers, journals, maps, photographs and drawings. Prehistoric items from the area and objects of the Basuto culture were displayed to showcase their customs and traditions.

The exhibition had been developed from the private collections of some of the fathers stationed here in the 19th century. From the early 1800s, missionaries were sent out to Africa to educate and convert local people to the Christian faiths. They also came to Lesotho.

Evangelical attempts

The missionaries from the Paris Evangelical Missionary Society had made their presence felt in Morija. Arriving here in 1833 to establish a small station, they immediately put their mark on the place by renaming it: "Our choice fell on one of the most beautiful valleys in the country [...] It bore the name of Makoarane, but we substituted that of Moriah, which expressed our gratitude to God for past mercies, and our confidence in him for the future."[11] As described in Genesis XXII of the Hebrew Bible, Abraham's aborted sacrifice of his son Isaac had taken place on Moriah Mountain. The fathers had no scruples disregarding local tradition.

The task of the missionaries turned out to be quite a challenge: "It was no easy matter to make these heathen – absorbed as they were with material things – feel the benefit they would derive, in a temporal point of view, from the diffusion of Christian doctrines." They aimed higher. At first, full of confidence of winning over king Moshoeshoe I, years later Father Casalis admitted in his memories: "We flattered ourselves that we should one day see the supreme chief of the country take up his abode with us; but after four years of expectation this hope had not been realized."[12] Never wavering in their unflinching endeavours, they carried on.

Missionaries did not come for short spells, they stayed for decades or even for life. The first to arrive was a group of three. Eugène Casalis remained in the country for 23 years. After two years in Morija, he moved to Thaba Bosiu to open a mission station close to Moshoeshoe's base. On many occasions he acted as the ruler's interpreter, adviser or informer, liaising between the chief, the mission, and colonial authorities. The other two were Thomas Arbousset, staying for 27 years, and Constant Gosselin, who died in Lesotho in 1872 after 39 years. David Frédéric Ellenberger arrived in Lesotho with his wife in 1860 and lived there for about 50 years. The missionary and artist François Maeder, also staying 50 years, left sketches of the local population. Adolphe and Adèle Mabille spent 34 years at Morija. She

---

[11] Eugène Casalis, The Basutos or twenty-three years in South Africa, p25.

[12] ibid., p15, p78.

was the Lesotho-born daughter of Eugène Casalis and was also involved in mission work; he translated the Bible into Sesotho, compiled a Sesotho-English dictionary, started a printing press and established a theological school.

While Moshoeshoe I, leader of the Basuto, allowed the foreigners to settle in his country, they acted as his inter-mediaries with the officials and the white settlers, who encroached on his land more and more. But in doing so, they got themselves between the lines.

When the Boers, in 1858, staged their first war against Moshoeshoe, they burnt almost all the mission's buildings to the ground, destroying Father Arbousset's valuable linguistic and historical research papers in the process. But they stopped short of also laying their hands on the church built by the missionaries soon after their arrival. When we were visiting, it looked just as it did at their time. The elongated red brick building had five windows each side and a red roof. The doors were open, and so we entered. The nave had a beautiful wooden ceiling, the polished benches had been well used over time by the faithful flock.

Ann was acquainted with the curator of the museum and the archives, Stephen Gill. He happened to be there and, glad to notice our interest in the place, showed us around. Besides of taking care of the exhibition, he was the author of a number of publications about Morija and Lesotho. Peter took the opportunity to buy his comprehensive book on the country's development from the Stone Age to the end of the 20th Century, *A Short History of Lesotho*.

The presence of a bunch of three foreigners caused a stir among the local children. As a habitual part of his travel routine, Peter went into the adjacent post office to buy several of Lesotho's beautiful stamps. About ten of the group came along to watch the procedure unfold. During the process of selecting, deciding, paying and collecting, they surrounded him, curiously following his every move. After the successful conclusion of the operation, they insisted on being photographed with him on the front steps of the building.

Catholic endeavours

Like Morija, Roma was also linked to French missionaries. Here the Roman Catholics established a mission in Tloutle and, just like their Protestant counterparts, immediately changed the traditional name to Roma upon arrival in 1862. Having tried in vain to evangelize white settlers and Zulu tribes, they came to Lesotho hoping to gain converts among the Basuto. Joseph Gérard stayed 61 years in Africa, Pierre Bernard died in Roma after 35 years in Africa, Bishop François Allard, the exception to the rule, returned to Europe after 20 years in Africa and only 10 years in the region.

In 1945, Pius XII College had been founded and was run by the Catholic Church and, following two name changes, the National University of Lesotho was opened in 1975. The faculties of law, agriculture, science, languages and others offer a wide range of subjects to study. The teaching, learning and research facilities have established the university over the years and are attracting students from many countries.

There was at least one primary school nearby with neatly dressed pupils in their uniforms playing and running around in the schoolyard. There were mainly girls. Boys were sent up the mountains to look after the family's animals, owing to the absence of their adult male relatives working in the South African mines. Therefore, girls could go to school and were more literate than boys. Besides three high schools, there were the headquarters of the Roman Catholic Church of Lesotho and a hospital, a few shops, a petrol station and numerous houses.

Visiting the chief's ruins

Next day we split. Peter went to a previous capital, Thaba Bosiu, while Ann and I headed for the present one, Maseru, in a shallow valley below the Maloti Mountains.

Peter had been booked by Ann for an excursion with a local guide to visit the ruins of the stronghold of the Basutos' famous chief Moshoeshoe I. They were the only visitors. After a climb up the slopes and rocks he and his guide arrived on the wide plateau.

It was easy to see why the Basuto leader had chosen the place. From a vantage point so high up, the surrounding area could be scanned and approaching enemies spotted. His fortress had withstood numerous attacks and campaigns to scale it by rival tribes and other assailants, like the Boers in 1865. Despite several attempts it was never taken in his lifetime, but destroyed later. Peter and his guide came to the place where the fortress once stood. There was not much left of his fortification, just some dilapidated walls. A particular tree was said to have shaded the elevated seat of the ruler. The resting place of the Great King and a few graves of other important dignitaries recalled their position in history. Moshoeshoe I had died in 1870 and was still remembered and revered as a great chief many generations later.

In June 1824, Moshoeshoe, then still a minor chief of the Mokoteli clan, had moved his base to the large and well-watered plateau to become the dominant chief of the Basuto. In the ensuing wars for supremacy he amassed huge herds of cattle not only by smart tribute systems and useful marriage alliances but also by raiding other tribes' livestock. In 1843, Moshoeshoe's claims to the land and his position as leader of the Basuto were recognized by the British. Soon after, his land was greatly reduced in another treaty in 1849. Many Boer families had invaded the borders in the 1830s, and Boer militia attacked Lesotho in March 1858 burning and destroying as they went. After a second war between the Basuto and the transgressing settlers in 1865-66, the British declared Lesotho a protectorate. They founded Maseru as the seat of the British administration for the then proclaimed Protectorate of Basutoland. After eighty years of British administration Lesotho gained independence in October 1966 and became a constitutional monarchy with Moshoeshoe II as King of Lesotho.

Acquiring a useful blanket

While Peter was exploring the chief's ruins, Ann and I travelled to Maseru to go to the bank and buy groceries. Established by the British governor in 1869 as the headquarters of the Cape Frontier Armed and Mounted Police, the city has been Lesotho's capital ever since. Well into the 1930s very much a centre for colonial officials and traders, by now it had developed into a modern town with office buildings, shops, stores, banks, markets, eateries, restaurants and hotels. Its urban aspirations were offset by its rural appearance with market stalls, battered pickups, street vendors and quite a few raggedly dressed people.

Before going to the bank and the shops, Ann warned me that a lot of patience and time was required to arrange anything, no matter what. So, I was prepared that it took ages to convert my travellers' cheque into cash. She, too, was queuing endlessly to withdraw money. Emphasizing her point, it also took a long time indeed to get through the checkout at the nearby supermarket. We did not have much in the shopping trolley, still things moved ever so slowly and could not be sped up.

In contrast, it was an easy process to buy a typical Lesotho blanket at the Frasers store, run by a South African whom Ann knew from her Sesotho language class. We walked in, had a chat with the manager, looked through the piles, and came out with a blanket for me. Conversation, selection and purchase were done in less than fifteen minutes.

The blanket turned out to be of good use to me a few years later. I had been commissioned to pick up a friend of Ann's at Heathrow Airport coming in from Washington. He used to live in Lesotho and was familiar with the customary attire of the country. He did not know me, I did not know him. Since our connection was Lesotho, the most appropriate way to find each other was the blanket. So, instead of holding a sign displaying his name, I awaited him in the arrivals hall covered in the blue blanket I had bought with Ann. People looked at me doubting whether I was in my right mind. Why would anyone wrap up in a very warm woollen blanket with a strange pattern on a stuffy hot summer's day. Scanning the waiting crowd, it did not take Ann's friend long to discover who in the crowd was there to meet him.

'This kind of blanket looks familiar. I guess you are my VIP limousine service?'

'So I am indeed. Welcome to Britain. Shall we give Ann a call.'

These ubiquitous blankets did not have a long Basuto tradition at all, they were going back just about a hundred years. When the discovery of diamond and gold mines in nearby South Africa had generated some buying power after the 1870s, trading companies like Frasers were quick to grasp the new opportunities. The traditional skin and fur covers were replaced by modern blankets, which were woven in the United Kingdom by Wormalds & Walker Mills of Drewsbury in Yorkshire, the largest manufacturer of woollen blankets in the world at the time, then shipped out to Lesotho and worn ever since.

Over the years, quality and patterns were changing. Attractive designs, varying from tribe to tribe and district to district, were developed and given Sesotho names. Used for formal occasions and events, the blankets became symbols of identity and prosperity.

On the way back to our meeting point with Peter, we passed a group of local girls walking by the roadside, whose naked upper bodies were smeared with a brown paste. As Ann explained, they had just gone through their initiation rites, held before they were admitted to adult society. The coming of age ceremonies marked their passing from childhood to womanhood and announced their eligibility for marriage. For a long time, rites of passage had been discouraged by the missionaries and the church, but in the changing political environment following independence people again turned to the traditional rituals.

Luckily and accidentally, we discovered Peter walking along the road all by himself, having been dumped by his friendly guide and his noble driver of a pick-up truck, a close relative of the king's.

'What happened, what are you doing here, it's not the point that was agreed?'

'This is where I should get out, they said with a smile.'

'They did not tell you more, give no reason?'

'No, they did not. That was it, and off they drove.'

'Why am I not surprised', was Ann's comment.

It was the first time Peter had a member of a royal household as a chauffeur. After this experience, I am not sure he would trust this variety of driver ever again.

We drove to the airport. Ann had arranged for a rental car, which was better suited than hers to get up the steep mountains. A 4×4 should be able to withstand the demands of the local roads. Registered in my name, it was now my turn to do the driving.

Harsh life on the mountains

Next day, we took the Land Rover for a drive to Marakabei via the Molimo Nthuse Pass. With a powerful engine, it was well equipped to climb up the steep gradients of mountain roads. With most of the country's unpaved roads in poor condition and only a fraction of the road network paved, the uphill gravel roads were not easy to negotiate. With all of Lesotho's land lying at an altitude above 1,000m, it is the highest country on the African continent; its mountains with peaks of more than 3,400m above sea level are among the highest in southern Africa.

The landscape we came through had a stunning magnificence about it, barren though it was. The spectacular scenery compensated us well for the inconvenience of getting to Lesotho in the first place: clean air, blue open skies, limitless space, endless horizons, hills and mountains, flat-topped koppies, deep valleys, and many terraced sorghum fields.

We could make out well-used narrow tracks along ridges and across slopes. Connecting the settlements in the valleys and on the mountains, they were used by horses, livestock and people alike. There were a few cattle herds, and many goats and sheep were widely scattered on the hills. The animals seemed to be roaming wherever they liked, the shepherds looking after them were nowhere to be seen.

The remote areas and highlands were sparsely populated. We did not see anyone and were wondering where they all were. The gravel road passed a few settlements of various sizes, a cluster of roundhouses marked a village while others comprised just a few of them with an occasional rectangular building. Walls were made of stones or mud with a roof covering of thatch. Single circular huts with their conical roof, the rondavels, were sprinkled across the slopes in the distance, the only sign of human habitation. One such dwelling struck me as it had the most stunning position on the ridge of a gently sloping hill with a valley on one side and the mountain on the other. Later, I sketched the view on my notepad.

There was traffic though, as everybody seemed to be on the road instead of at home. Vehicles had to negotiate potholes, animals and people. Minibuses packed to the rafters with humans and poultry made their way to their destination. Trucks brought goods and food to the remote villages. There were less than a handful of private cars.

Barefoot on icy snow

If not by bus, men travelled on horseback, their main mode of transport in the country's difficult terrain. Every now and then we met small groups of horsemen on the road, some with packhorses or donkeys. They were clad in beautiful blankets, looking most majestic and highly dignified.

Women, who could not afford the bus fare, were forced to use a different method. With transport and money not available, they had no option but to use their legs - whatever the weather and the distance.

We saw a group of colourfully dressed women walking with bare feet in single file along the road. With proud grace they were balancing heavy loads on their heads.

'They are beautiful. How do they manage to carry their basket without it falling over?'

'All women have been practising from childhood, so they are used to it', explained Ann. 'I am always amazed how long and far they are able to walk like that. You and I, we would not be able to do that.'

'What a workout', preferring my own variety which was less strenuous.

Perhaps they were heading for a place to trade their goods, or finding a job to earn some money, or just visiting. On account of the great poverty, men, but mainly women and children were used to walk without shoes no matter what the circumstances and conditions were. Two women recount their experience.

One woman describes how she walked about 70km together with her young daughter: "I would leave Marakabei to come to Roma, maybe to come to see my mother, we always went together, walking by foot with no shoes."[13] While walking, the mother had an infant on her back, whom

---

[13]Kendall K.L., Singing away the hunger, p73.

the six year old took on her own back in order to let her mother rest while still walking on.

Even when it was severely cold with temperatures far below 0°C, some still were out and about: "The Maluti Mountains began to get rough. Steep, rocky, real rough. Worse still, it was snowing that day. The air was chilly and freezing to the bone-marrow, more so when we were wrapped in tattered blankets and had no shoes on our feet." Regardless of such atrocious weather, they had to carry on in order to reach their relatives' rondavel. "Slowly we began to climb those cold, slippery and uncompromising mountains. [...] We struggled up the mountains in a numbing temperature. I could not feel my toes. Our faces were stung by the chilling winter winds. A vicious icy snow pelted us in the face."[14] When they did arrive, the baby one of them had carried on her back, was dead.

Frozen herdboys

We parked to admire the view across the valleys and mountains. Two very young herdboys appeared from nowhere, sat down on the kerbside and observed us in silence. They wore sandals and a woollen blanket. In summer or winter, this was more or less what they would wear throughout the year, never mind the weather or the temperature. They had nothing else as Ann explained.

These were the boys who had to spend their days on the mountains, taking care of the family's herds, in sun or rain, in ice or snow. With the men of most families away in South Africa to support their wives and children, the task of tending the animals fell to the sons of the family.

Lads like them could be treated pitilessly if an elder of the community was so inclined: "In July the water was

---

[14]Kendall K.L., Basali !, p31-32.

frozen in the streams. [...] He took a big stick to break the ice, and he put the ice-cold water in the basin, and he forced the children to wash in the icy water. [...] If they didn't wash, he would beat them with a big stick." After this kind of encouragement they were sent out "to watch the cattle with nothing to wear but their little thin blankets in that cold and snow. My boys were sick; they fell asleep; and some of the sheep got away. When the children woke up and saw what had happened, they were afraid to come home. They know he will beat them." Suffering that kind of violent abuse, children were crushed into obedience with no way out of a time-honoured system.

With frost and ice, heavy snowfall and freezing winds, temperatures in winter in the highlands can plummet to minus 20°C. Still, the boys had to stay on the mountains, without suitable protection or cover of any kind, and often even without enough food. Some hardly survived the conditions: "They looked up and down, until they found him under a bush [...], kneeling and curled up round like a bowl. He is freezing. His skin is turning white, like paper; his eyes are closed, he can't talk [...] his bones are cold and stiff, like a dead person. He can't move. They carry him on their shoulder like a frozen lamb."[15] Two days later the boy was forced to return to his herd.

The young herdsmen had full responsibility for all animals entrusted to their care, and they were punished if some of them went missing or were stolen. With frequent stock theft, they were often threatened by armed criminals who took their animals, sold the stolen cattle, donkeys, or sheep to South Africa or to butcheries along the border. The pressure to keep their herd together and the fear of punishment were more frightening than death in the mountains.

---

[15]Kendall K.L., Singing away the hunger, p86-87, 95.

A rough and tough childhood

As the social standing and wealth of the family was measured in the number of livestock they owned, as many animals as possible or practicable were acquired. But they had to be taken care of. Most men were away in Gauteng, and so the remaining male members of a family were boys. As tradition and custom dictated, for ages they have been used as guards for the sheep, donkeys, goats or cows. The task of tending the livestock of a family fell to the sons from the age of five, or even younger, to around sixteen. Not necessarily were the herdboys the own sons of the family, orphaned children or sons of impoverished families were also taken on in that role. Whether they were still young children or young adults, they were compelled to go up to the remote pastures. Fulfilling their obligation the boys had to stay in the mountains for long periods, even months at a stretch.

There they had to remain with only animals for company, rarely other humans. Most of the seasons, they spent their time isolated and entirely on their own. Except with other boys in the same situation, they had no opportunity to socialize with others. Away from their families, there was no one to look after them. They had very little food, if any, no assistance in case of injury or ill-health, no help of any kind. These boys had and still have only little prospect of economic advance, they will be shepherds all their lives or end up working in the South African mines just as their fathers and uncles.

Herding was not only seen as necessary work but also as a rite of passage from boyhood to manhood by taking on responsibility for other living beings, defending the herds and surviving solitude and severe conditions.

Alone on the far-away grazing grounds on the mountains, the child shepherds had no chance of gaining an education, unlike their sisters who stayed in the villages. However, in recent years a special program for the herdboys has been launched, and almost a dozen night schools have been established across the highlands to address their isolation, illiteracy and their vulnerable situation in the mountainous regions. They learn life skills and are given guidance on drug and alcohol abuse, anger management, basics of agriculture and other topics. They also receive advice on their rights. A health outreach program has also been established to deal with general health issues such as HIV, diabetes, or dentistry among others. The Child Protection and Welfare Bill and the National Strategic Plan on Vulnerable Children attempt to improve the general situation of Lesotho's boys in particular, but also of the girls; however, implementation and enforcement leave room for improvement.

With that background about the boys' lives, the wonderful landscape in front of us lost a bit of its impressive beauty. Since age-old customs and widespread poverty in

Lesotho will only gradually ease the hardship of the young herdsmen, we could only hope that some progress might lessen their burden in the future.

We did not get as far as Marakabei but had to return to Roma, since William was expected for a brief get-together in Lesotho. We found him in the parking lot, napping in his car after a five hour drive from Pretoria.

From cart to airplane

Next morning William, Peter, and I headed for Semonkong in the mountains. Leaving Ann at the university and William's precious car close to her flat, hoping it would not be too tempting for thieves, we jumped into the sturdy 4×4. As the registered driver, I got behind the steering wheel, not knowing what to expect.

A bumpy challenge not for the faint-hearted

Right outside the campus we turned left for the road from where we had to turn back on our first excursion with Ann. While the ascent had beaten the abilities of her car, it was still not easy for the offroader. Even with plenty of horse-power the engine worked hard to crawl up the hill.

For about just 10km the road had been paved only to continue as a gravel road up the steep mountain. Soon, climbing up to almost 2800m, the road became a dirt road with deep potholes and wide creeks; conditions that called for rather stout-hearted driving skills. In fact, in places the so-called road was quite demanding on the driver's speed of reaction and on the car's stamina and goodwill. Thanks to the ground clearance of the Land Rover, the vehicle did not suffer any damage along bends left and right or through dents and puddles. I had to make sudden swerves around a variety of obstacles: rocks, horsemen, cattle, people, donkeys, with overcrowded minibuses and overloaded trucks contributing to the trials.

Our intestines were seriously tested. Jolted, shaken and stirred, we finally arrived on the high plateau where, at 2275m above sea level, Semonkong was located.

Eventually, in the distance, houses dotted about the brownish horizon indicated the location of the village. Semonkong at the end of the road was the only major settlement in these parts. Its buildings were scattered over a large area on the wide plains. This was the only place of trade serving the mountain region. A number of dirt tracks fanned out in various directions, reflecting the central significance of the village. People, animals and goods were distributed from here all over the district.

Intrepid entrepreneurs

A settlement so remote had never been easy to service. Owing to the demanding terrain of the mountains, transport was difficult and time consuming. But a few daring individuals had the guts and business sense to establish trading stations in just such spots. Besides a number of Indian traders and other Europeans like the Thorn family of the Roma Trading Post, the best known were the pioneering Fraser brothers, Donald and Douglas Henry.

Descending from a British wool merchant of London, the Frasers recognized great business opportunities in Lesotho. They were not put off by any difficulties obtaining licences from local chiefs or by immense distances and isolated locations. Opening new stores or taking over some that already existed, they started a network of stations in the late 19th century, trading and selling anything from wool and grain and animals to nails and ploughs and building material. From their headquarters in Wepener, Orange Free State, they established a reliable and well-run organisation with stores not only in far away sites but also in towns like Maseru or cities like Johannesburg.

Over the space of more than a hundred years, the stations of the brothers have grown into a large business, most of the time managed by members of the family. With many illustrating anecdotes, the story of the Frasers up to the 1970s is narrated by Christopher Danziger in *A Trader's Century*. It seems the modified company has survived into the 21st century, evolving from modest beginnings to moderate success into a very successful venture.

Besides Marakabei and Morija, Semonkong was one of the bigger stations. Opened in 1938, it began operations with a storage shed, a mud hut as the manager's house, stables and a shop. Initially, transport was made by horse, donkey or ox-waggon. Where the terrain allowed to make an airstrip as in Semonkong, the outlaying stations were supplied from the air, thus greatly facilitating transport, storage and general logistics and making life easier for the traders and for the population.

Whether a plane with stores had recently landed, we could not make out. When we arrived at Semonkong the place was buzzing. Trucks, busses, pick-ups and horses had converged on a large open space. Children running around among the hustle and bustle, women with loads on their heads awaiting departure, uninvolved people wearing conical grass hats looking on, men wrapped in their blankets watching the procedures, magnificent riders on beautiful horses displaying an air of grandeur.

Avoiding any offence, we stayed well back, observing all the excitement from a distance.

Since we planned to go back to Pretoria later in the day, we could not stay for very long but had to get back to Roma.

I steeled myself for the return drive. Descending most of the time, the way back was much easier. Yet, the number of potholes had not decreased.

William's car had not been touched.

Back to the North

Ann and I returned the rental car. Not surprising to her, the Avis lady had not turned up at the agreed time at the airport counter. There was no one to give the keys to or inspect the vehicle. We had just given up and were about to leave when she appeared thirty minutes late, without giving a reason why we had been kept waiting. Seasoned, Ann only shrugged.

We left Roma in the evening. On the bridge into South Africa, Basuto women were selling mealies. Just after the crossing on our left, clad in their blankets, Basuto men were waiting for transport to the mines as on the night we arrived.

Travelling through Bethlehem and Frankfort, two of many farming towns in the region, we arrived in William's house in Pretoria at midnight after a five hour journey. Considering the outward journey had taken us over sixteen hours, a mere five was just a short hop.

The dogs welcomed us back enthusiastically.

Next day we prepared for our departure to Britain. Late afternoon, William gave us a lift to Johannesburg airport. Two years later we saw him again, in the southern part of Kruger National Park.

Like the provinces in South Africa, the airport has undergone several name changes in its sixty year history. Until 1994 is was called Jan Smuts Airport after the twice Prime Minister of the Union of South Africa between 1919 and 1948. It was Johannesburg International Airport until 2006, when it was renamed Oliver Tambo Airport to honour the twice president of the African National Congress and friend and comrade of Nelson Mandela. He also has an airport named after him, in Praia in the Cape Verde Islands.

High in the air, I dreamed of elephants and gazelles, of mountains and herdboys, but also of vicious dogs that were so friendly, they did not even bark.

'The Spirit of the Wild is quick to assert her supremacy'

In the Bushveld

of Kruger National Park

An email arrived from my husband: would I care for another trip to South Africa. Definitely and of course I would, and so two comfortable airline seats were booked.

Peter was to attend a conference in Berg-en-Dal at the southern fringes of the Kruger National Park. A perfect excuse for me to take a break and jump on the plane to JNB.

Intense African sunshine welcomed us at the gate in Johannesburg, and we brightened up quickly after the overnight flight from London.

We knew that we did not have to make our own way to Krugerpark, everything was being taken care of for us. Transportation from the airport straight to the conference venue had been arranged for all the delegates, which was very convenient indeed. In the arrivals hall, we were met by a conference assistant who informed us that the chartered coach was to wait for everybody and therefore not due to leave before midday. As we were the first to arrive, we had to linger at the airport until all the other international and national delegates had landed.

With a few hours to hang around at the airport, we set up camp on the seats in the arrivals hall. Whiling away the time we explored the shops, watched people, read the newspapers, took a stroll outside in the sun and the traffic fumes. Luckily, a stall with boerewors and biltong was close-by. By noon all the remaining delegates had arrived, and the coach left for Krugerpark.

I sat back and tried not to feel tired. In fact, getting to see new landscapes that opened a window into the past, I enjoyed the ride. Contrary to a few of my fellow passengers, who quickly succumbed to the effect of their flight.

Travelling through the Transvaal

Heading in an easterly direction on the N12 and N4, the road to Mozambique, we came through Gauteng und Mpumalanga, once the Province of the Transvaal.

The area we travelled through was one of the regions, which had been fought over in several wars in the second half of the 19th century. A number of towns recalled the time when the British, the Boers, various settlers, and local tribes were involved in skirmishes, confrontations, sieges, and battles over land and dominance.

The districts were also important because of the construction of a railway link from the Transvaal to the Indian Ocean before the turn to the 20th century.

Railway depots and battle grounds

Part of the N4 followed the railway line from Pretoria to Lourenço Marques in Portuguese East Africa. Most of the towns strung along it came into being when the track was built in the 1890s, connecting the interior with the Indian Ocean port. With the development of the goldfields and the growing industrialization, demand for better logistics increased. The well-used trade routes had to be improved to offer more efficiency.

The coach passed a few towns on the railway line. Many a the place name evoked the Boer presence in the area, and by implication, in South Africa as a whole. Founded and named as Nazareth by the Boer settlers in the 1860s, Middelburg was a coal-mining town with steel plants and agricultural production as well as many churches. Having destroyed their farms and their cattle during the Second Anglo-Dutch or Boer war, in 1901 the British rounded up the Boers into camps where hundreds of them died. The

British Fort recalled the period, and a cemetery remembered the dead, Boer forces and British soldiers alike.

One of the towns we were passing, Waterval Boven, now Emgwenya, on the edge of the Drakensberg Escarpment, had been a railway supply depot in 1895 for the new track to Delagoa Bay. Near the town, the road descended onto the lowveld and ran along the Elands River. Here, in the autumn of 1900, the Boers had attacked one of the British stations that guarded vital supplies. Today, the river is more famous for its gorges, rapids and dams than for previous warfare. The dramatic scenery of its waterfalls has become a destination for rock climbing. The area is also well known for farming, fishing and tourism.

After the Elands had joined the Crocodile River, we came through Nelspruit, now Mbombela, administrative and business centre of the lowveld and capital of Mpumalanga, or Eastern Transvaal. During the construction of the railway line, the place was used as a depot for stock, material and men. Its location in the fertile valley of the river had made the town a trading hub for the surrounding fruit and nut growing area.

Fruits and canes

Commercial farming of sub-tropical produce and fresh crops had started in the region about a hundred years ago. Fruit growing operations developed into one of the key economic sectors in South Africa, and the country has become one of the leading suppliers to the global market. Grapefruit, lemons, oranges, mango, banana, avocado as well as macadamia and pecan nuts were cultivated, harvested, graded, packed in large factories and sent out to their destinations.

Spreading as far as the eye could see, the immense orange plantations displaying the Outspan brand label were particularly impressive. I was struck by the immaculate tidiness of the estate, a picture of perfection. Trees covered in their sweet fruits were planted in very neat very long parallel rows. The whole farm looked as if it had been dusted, washed, cleaned, hoovered, shampooed and blow-dried just a minute ago.

By contrast, the camps on the supply route to and from the goldfields, where the oxen teams were outspanned for the night, would have looked at the Outspan fields with envy, considering that their impromptu places consisted of a wild assortment of sheds, huts, waggons, animals and heaps of stores. The rough tracks for waggons and riders were a far cry from the easy alleys to accommodate the plantations' machinery and equipment. The idea of the name is said to go back to a fruit label created by Sir Percy Fitzpatrick, who was once a member of the outspan complement. Anyhow, naming the brand after the outspan stations in the bushveld is meant to honour the labours of the toiling transport crews in the 19th century.

Krokodilpoort and Kaapmuiden were some of the small towns that had sprung up with the railway line on its way East. On a smaller scale than Nelspruit, these places were also involved in growing exotic fruit.

Further down the road, the large area around Malelane, now Malalane, was another productive area with more processing plants and undulating fields of sugarcane. There were the mills, refineries and silos of Transvaal Sugar Limited, turning the green cane stalks into raw or refined sugar, syrups and molasses. Starting out as a railroad depot in 1895 like Waterval Boven, 120 years on, the small settlement of Malalane has developed into a substantial centre of South Africa's sugar producing industry. Bordering the national park, large plantations of the tall grasses along the valley of the Crocodile River promised a rich harvest.

About 60km from the border with Mozambique, shortly after Malelane, the coach turned left and headed into the Krugerpark.

Approaching the gate complex, I thought about the beginnings of the park.

From game reserve to national park

In 1880, a proposition to establish a game reserve had already been contemplated, but only in 1898 at last a game reserve was proclaimed by President Paul Kruger. It was called Sabi (modernized Sabie) Reserve. However, it was the commitment of a spirited warden and a group of adventurous rangers that turned the plan into reality.

Without the efforts of Major (and later Colonel) James Stevenson-Hamilton in the early 1900s, there would probably be no Kruger National Park. Explorer, big game hunter and ex-cavalry officer, his aim was to protect wild animals from extermination by white and tribal hunters by establishing a sanctuary.

He was the active force in transforming the wilderness into a game reserve and ultimately into a national park, a concept perceived by some as a crazy idea: "Of course it was looked on by all natives and by most white men as folly, and myself as rather a harmful kind of interfering lunatic." His attitude towards the animals was regarded as very odd by one of his attendants: "When he saw a zebra standing so close that I could have hit it with a stone, he only looked at it. Truly, he is quite mad!" [16]

---

[16]South African Eden, p57.

Dealing with adversities of many kinds

Major Stevenson-Hamilton had to face complications and opposition to the project from various quarters. Being considered somewhat insane by some did not always help his cause. But he proceeded against much resistance and prejudice. When appointed head warden of the reserve, he had his hands full with multiple tasks.

He had to get to know the wilderness, find suitable rangers, define districts, coordinate operations, stop the trade in game skin and meat, and prevent the native peoples and white hunters from continuing to deplete the animals.

Ownership of land had to be sorted out for hundreds of private, company or government owned farms as well as uninhabited properties and unallocated spaces. Also the problem of winter grazers occupying government land and squatters appropriating estates that had taken their fancy had to be addressed. There were also conflicting land, grazing and mining concessions to deal with. And there were those who insisted on shooting the wild animals regardless, and those who complained of being deprived of trading, hunting and prospecting opportunities. Envy and jealousy as well as resentment from various sides at times made life difficult for the new warden. Laws and regulations conceived at office desks in Pretoria were often issued without much thought as to their viability.

Bureaucratic concerns were one thing, but critical health scares were quite another.

Serious danger for humans and animals

Far away from any doctor and with very little medical supplies available to them, the men had to rely on self-help and their own ingenuity and just suffer through minor mishaps or major disasters. Injuries, accidents and worst of all malaria had to be dealt with as circumstances and available means allowed which were rather poor.

Almost from the start infectious diseases were affecting the rangers and their animals. Bilharzia, dysentery and malaria and its often deadly complication called blackwater fever as well as horse-sickness took their toll. Caused by a parasite, malaria is transmitted by an infected mosquito, whereas horse-sickness is caused by a virus and spread by a midge. Both infections occur mainly in the wet season and, even today, have not been eradicated.

Brandy to treat ill humans

When malaria or other infections hit, in many cases drugs like quinine and phenacetin taken with hot whiskey were useful to reduce pain and fever. The dreaded symptoms are headaches, high fever with sweating and violent shivering occurring in cycles over many days if not weeks. One of Major Stevenson-Hamilton's bouts of the ailment lasted several months. At times, the rangers in the wilderness ran out of their limited stock of medicine, and there was nothing they could do to help their mates. If not even quantities of alcohol were helpful, they had to let them die. Occasionally, however, with an extraordinary amount of effort lives could be saved.

In particular when struck down with blackwater fever, patients were soon at death's door and rarely recovered. Not all were as lucky as Sergeant Harry Wolhuter. When he was down with an acute attack and desperately weak, he was carried by his men 60km through the bush to the Selati train track, put on a pump trolley and transported another 80km to the nearest hospital and then sent on farther to a hospital ship in Delagoa Bay. There, convalescent but contracting a relapse of ordinary malaria, despite his protests, he was subjected to a treatment of being rubbed down with ice several times. When he got not better but even worse, the medical staff finally accepted the inefficiency of their regime and gave in to his demands for the well tested cure. Wolhuter improved immediately when he applied his own bush-proven methods of analgesic and alcohol.

Opium to cure sick animals

With no veterinary support anywhere near, their animals were also suffering terribly. Besides enduring injuries caused by falls or attacks by wild animals or other misfortunes, horses, mules and donkeys were struck by horse-sickness. With a high mortality rate, the disease affected the respiratory and cardiovascular system of the animals. With no medication within reach and their only other option letting the animals die, the resourceful rangers came up with their own method of treating their unfortunate companions. Occasionally, a strong dose of laudanum, an opium tincture, was administered to a sick horse which, with luck, was cured within days. Losing their horses was a heavy blow to the rangers. Those who had survived previous attacks of the sickness were to a great degree resistant for life and did not die even if afflicted by periodical recurrences. The so-called salted horses were sought after and not easy to get hold of.

In case of critical wounds and grave injuries to their animals, or to their fellow rangers for that matter, the men did what ever they could to save them. Ranger Harold Trollope once operated on a disembowelled donkey that had been attacked by a lion. Cold-blooded, he pushed back the entrails and stitched up the poor animal. The brave donkey survived his horrendous ordeal thanks to the surgical skills of his handler.

Solitude in the bush

Besides dealing with dangers, injuries and diseases, the rangers had to bear the effects of loneliness and remoteness; they had to be of a stable frame of mind to cope with their isolated situation in that wilderness. In their lonely post they were without social contacts for long stretches of time, except occasionally meeting up with their fellow rangers or running into them when out on patrol. However, some of them had farms not too far from their camps which they visited when their duties allowed, like Rangers Trollope and Wolhuter. Yet, in the bush they were on their own. In the vastness of land there were not many whites to keep company with. If there were any humans, it was local or roaming tribes who, however, had different goals and attitudes than the men of the reserve.

Their only companions for long periods were their horses and their dogs as well as donkeys and mules for pack animals. At times, Game Ranger Wolhuter kept a rather wild assortment of pets to soften his existence: a bushpig, a dingo pub, a young warthog, a number of lion cubs and a variety of small animals he found abandoned in the bush or were given to him. Antoinette was the temporary pet of Ranger Trollope, she was one of three tiny lion cubs he nursed after the death of their mother; she still recognized him many years after he had given her away.

Their solitary existence not only reflected their isolated compound in a remote corner of the wilderness, but also the difficulty of communicating with their fellow rangers and the outside world. Riding on horseback or walking cross-country was the only way of getting in touch with the nearest camp or settlement in the early years. Often, it took many days to reach anyone. The Selati Railway line, built for the goldfields in the 1890s, helped connecting the rangers with civilization, but most stations were too far away from the tracks. In the 1920s, roads were constructed linking the sections and making their days easier.

When sickness and isolation conspired, their remoteness became even more pronounced. Since most of the rangers lived far out in the bush, no one would know if they had fallen ill, had an accident or even died. It would take time or chance for someone to discover what had happened. Their remote post did not allow for a family to live there, but there was a rare exception, which ended tragically. When one of the rangers who had his family with him, died in the 1920s, it fell to his wife to bury her husband herself. Major Stevenson-Hamilton was informed about the death by a messenger who reached him after running night and day through lion country for twenty-four hours.

Rewards from nature for exceptional men

Life in the bush was hard, rough, dangerous, lonely and without any creature comforts to speak of. Attuned to the unpredictability of their situation and believing in themselves and trusting their capabilities, the rangers relied on their audacity, their courage, their horsemanship and their prowess with the gun. Lesser men could not have survived in the wild at the time.

Notwithstanding the risks that came with the territory and their responsibilities, the land and the animals made up for their struggle and hardship. Game Ranger Sergeant Harry Wolhuter describes how his views on the challenges facing them were changing: "In the course of our duties it became more and more interesting, and we obtained a great deal of pleasure learning the habits of the different kinds of game, in whose welfare and increase we soon began to foster a quite fatherly pride and care." Most of the rangers were relatively young, daring and fearless and they considered "the price levied by the exacting nature of the conditions worthwhile". The remoteness of their location and the solitude of their post also had positive aspects: "In addition to this, the secluded and virgin nature of the country, with its extremely few white residents, made of it a little world in itself where there was always much to explore and the possibility of new things to discover."[17] He, together with Major Stevenson-Hamilton and many of his fellow rangers, put up with bites of the anopheles mosquito and attacks by lions for more than forty years.

Looking back on their achievements, Major Stevenson-Hamilton with great respect reflected on the subtle and profound influence of their surroundings on themselves: "Few, however, can sojourn long within the unspoilt wilderness of a game sanctuary [...] without absorbing its atmosphere; the Spirit of the Wild is quick to assert her supremacy, and no man of any sensibility can resist her."[18]

The men of the first reserve recognized the overwhelming force that nature's wonders had on their efforts but also on their tribulations. The magic spell of their environment gave them strength and determination to meet the demands of their task. The dedication and care of the rangers for the land and its plants and animals they had taken responsibility for never waned.

---

[17]Memories of a game ranger, p117.
[18]South African Eden, p154.

Mission accomplished

With the conservation efforts and the unwavering perseverance of the warden and the rangers, the vision to establish a nature reserve became a reality. And so, after almost thirty years of hardship, setbacks and triumphs, the new park opened its gates.

The original Sabi Reserve had been extended with more land added over the years and, in 1927, opened to the public as the Kruger National Park. In 1935 just two dozen visitors were counted, in 1946 the number had increased to over 38,000, in the fiscal year of 2016/2017 the park attracted more than 1.8 million people.[19] With ever more people and cars coming to the park, and its infrastructure being developed and extended over the decades, I am not sure the first warden would approve wholeheartedly.

The rangers' job, at the time, other than preserving wildlife and nature, entailed educating people. A conversation between Ranger Wolhuter and a female visitor illustrates the point. After enlightening her that wildebeest did not eat small bucks, she persisted: "But the giraffes eat wildebeeste [sic], don't they? and when I corrected her and told her that the giraffe browse off the leaves of the trees, she expressed her pleasure that they didn't all eat each other!"[20] Today, it is unlikely that questions of this nature would be put to a ranger, given that plenty of information is widely available on television and the web.

We were to spend several days in the south western end of the region that was once the Sabi Game Reserve. We were exploring the region the first warden and his rangers had been travelling through on horseback accompanied by

---

[19]Figures according to *African Journal of Hospitality, Tourism and Leisure*, Vol 7, 2018, p21. More recent statistics could not be found.

[20]Memories of a game ranger, p255.

their dogs. The waggon route taken by the transport riders from the goldfields of the highveld around Lydenburg via the lowveld down to Lourenço Marques in Portuguese East Africa on the coast of the Indian Ocean ran through that area.

On many occasions we were criss-crossing the faded tracks of the ox-waggons and the rangers' riding trails; driving around the modern tarmac and dirt roads, in some sense, we were retracing their steps.

In the Berg-en-Dal camp

Malelane Gate is one of the main entrances into Kruger National Park. After a brief stop at the welcoming building with its large thatched roof, the coach made its way to Berg-en-Dal, about 12km from the southern perimeter. At 4:30pm at last, around twenty hours after having left home, we arrived at our destination. Some of the people in the coach had missed all the sights of the whole trip. Flown in from Japan, Australia or the US, they slept soundly in their seats and were reluctant to wake up. We knew how it feels being jetlagged and only wishing to sleep. Luckily, this time, we were almost on the same time zone.

We met up with William who had booked us into his quarters. It was a spacious family cottage with two good sized bedrooms with plenty of warm blankets, a bathroom, a large lounge with sliding glass doors opening to the patio, and a kitchen area with a slow cooker and a large freezer. A generous stock of sugar, salt, bread, eggs, drinks, as well as boerewors and biltong on the kitchen shelves suggested our friend had raided his Pretoria larder. With a house mate like that there was little danger we would experience deficiencies of any kind. Our contribution was a copious supply of two varieties of loose tea, which I refuse to travel without and all of us were sharing.

Bravado in the pond

The conference could wait; we decided and set out to inspect the compound.

Opened in February 1984, the Berg-en-Dal camp was the southernmost in the Krugerpark. Its name reflected the topography of the area, with the Afrikaans name berg en dal meaning hill and dale. The highest elevation was just over 800m. Its natural bushveld vegetation and habitat has been left largely untouched. Groups of trees and clusters of shrubs alternated with sweeps of tall grass. An area of high rainfall in summer, the scenic landscape was dry when we were there in mid winter.

Dotted among many trees and shrubs, remnants of the original woodlands, there were more than twenty cottages of various sizes and shapes. A swimming pool invited the patrons to take a refreshing plunge after many hours of strenuous game spotting. At a petrol station the dusty cars could be filled up after a long day's drive.

The main building housed the conference centre, the administration, the reception and the restaurant. There was also a shop that stocked basic food supplies and beverages, anti-malaria medication was also available.

Behind the complex, a platform offered views across the small lake that formed when a dam in the Matjulu River was built. A few tree skeletons in the lake reminded us that beneath the body of water was a valley, which had been flooded for the benefit of the lodge.

From the benches on the platform we enjoyed watching the creatures coming here for a dip or a drink. Some had made the lake their home. While we were there, a few crocodiles were basking on the sand. Motionless but alert they pretended to sleep. A party of terrapins was resting on the warm rocks, a snack probably too insignificant for the neighbours. A troupe of skittish monkeys, a potential meal, were chasing each other above our heads in the trees, overhanging the water and the viewing area. They all appeared to be on a friendly footing with everyone else. Or so it seemed.

'How are you getting on with each other?', putting the question to all of them from my seat.

'I'll show you.' The biggest of the crocs only opened his huge snout, exhibiting rows of sharp teeth for a convincing answer.

The small terrapins declared, 'We are the smallest, but we are nearly as old as that reptile. We hiss in unisono, if our neighbours do not respect our ancestry which also goes back millions of years.'

'We are faster than those archosauria', boasted the long-tailed clan, feeling superior to anyone on their airy perch high above them.

Birds in the near bushes, ancient as they were too, left it to them outshining each other. They were not of the bragging sort.

'Since you are all on the best of terms, I don't need to worry about you eating each other, or do I', recalling the remark Ranger Wolhuter had heard from a concerned lady visitor.

'They are all rather big-mouthed, except the one with the big mouth', Peter murmured. 'They all better behave, playing to the gallery is not always without risks.'

Animosities and rivalries did not disturb the peace in the competitive waters too much. Outdone and feeling ridiculous in such illustrious company, I retreated, considering their pride of ancient genealogy and my own family tree going back a mere seven hundred years. I was not even fit to sit here.

The croc only sent me a meaningful sideways glance, shutting his jaws with a frightful crack. The small turtles stood tall, unimpressed by his display of brute force; they were also prehistoric anyway. Even though they were not that ancient, the monkeys looked haughtily down on everyone, using their branches as a trampoline, high-flying to the canopy. What an arrogant bunch you are, I felt, overdoing your histrionics so preposterously.

In the near distance, the hills of the surrounding woodlands appeared brown and grey under the blue skies. The opposite bank was grassy, sandy and sunny at the lower end of the dam. Further upriver either side, dense green shrubs and a few trees were lining the shaded water's edge.

We left and took a trail leading down close to the river and further along the boundary of the camp. For obvious reasons a high electrified fence had been erected, keeping unwanted visitors away from those booked-in.

Animals were shut out, and people were locked in.

Encounters with the animals of the veld

The only exit-entry into the camp was through the main gate which was guarded by an armed post. His job was to prevent the lions from reconnoitring the camp, not to let any impatient game spotters sneak out before opening time, and to fine stragglers for disregarding the rules when returning past closing time.

We passed through the gate a number of times, sometimes a little late, most of the time on time. We ventured outside the camp as often as the conference schedule allowed, armed with binoculars, camera, biltong, bottles of water and plenty of patience and curiosity.

Once again we were taught that there is no need to search for animals, since they show up at their leisure anyway. Proof of William's dictum was given us right on the first morning.

Sleepy hyenas and busy fowls

Since we had come to Berg-en-Dal to watch animals, never mind the conference, jumping out of bed early was the order of the day. Given the environment and the expectations coming with it, getting up was not too difficult after all. With the opening of the gates the three of us set out.

Ten minutes after leaving the camp we encountered two spotted hyenas loitering in a bend of the road. They were completely unconcerned about the approaching car. They seemed to expect morning visitors, and we obliged. At a distance of less than 10m, the car stopped and the engine was switched off. Against the rules, the windows were opened, just a little. Thus, we could listen to the sounds of the bush and take in the fresh air of the early hours of the day.

We sat in silence, all eyes and ears. One of the magic moments among wildlife.

We heard their sounds of communicating and the sand crunch under their paws. One of them was very curious and approached the car, looking at us, sniffing and pondering. His nose did not like what it discovered, and he walked away to nearby bushes to take a well deserved mornings' nap. His mate was not interested at all and bedded down in the middle of the road. He might have just felt the need to sleep off last night's scavenging expedition. He did not move when William restarted the engine, probably dreaming of yesterday's hunting adventure.

At a crossroads we saw a graceful cheetah walking in the tall grass. A couple of other cars were also there observing the unperturbed cat. Binoculars, cameras, cars and excited people not in the least minding, the elegant creature strolled casually across the warm tarmac road. There were more important things to consider than a few fuel-emitting objects. The grass closed over the beauty, the cat disappeared from sight into nearby bushes.

Driving along, we came to a sizeable flock of colourful helmeted guineafowls, attractive birds with blue-greyish feathers with white spots. They occupied the whole width of the road without any intention of running for cover or giving way. We had to stop.

'Good morning; sorry to interrupt, but would you mind?'

'Good morning; sorry, we are busy as you can see. This is a perfect patch for having breakfast.'

'Well, then we have to keep you company, if that is acceptable to you.'

'Please do. We like to have guests. Temporarily.'

They gave us a benign glance, when the vehicle came to a standstill next to them and the engine was switched off. So close to their activities, the car did not irritate them at all, in fact they could not care less. Tolerating our presence, the fowls kept scratching in the soil and the sand, foraging for insects and seeds on the road and in the grass.

When the birds felt it was time for us to leave their table, they moved to either side of the road to let us pass. We waved them good bye.

Returned to the camp, we attended the conference for a few hours.

Disgusted jackals

Late afternoon we joined a three hour night drive in an open-sided safari vehicle organised by the camp guides. This was the only way to drive around in the wilderness at night, as private cars were not allowed outside the camp after dark. Since the evening promised to turn cold very soon, plenty of blankets were provided for the guests to wrap in. Torches were also distributed. When the last of the fifteen passengers had arrived, the tour began.

The first port of call was Matjulu Waterhole not far from the camp. Here the car came to a halt and the engine was turned off. With dusk gradually progressing into dark, the guide switched on the searchlights on top of her vehicle. We were waiting for a particular white rhino that was in the habit of coming here every day at about this hour. Ears perked and eyes searching, we stared into the vegetation, but saw and heard nothing.

The rhino's time-keeping was immaculate. Two minutes after the guide's announcement the massive animal burst forth from the scrubs. Like a ghost all of a sudden he appeared out of nowhere. We had not heard him approach, not even breaking twigs which his enormous body pushed aside. Like a Hollywood celebrity, he was used to being in the spotlight and attracting the crowds. Contrary to his movie counterparts, the rhino did not crave all the attention, waiting for the cameras to roll. In fact, he did not care at all for the vehicle and beams. Only interested in a sundowner, he headed straight for the water. After a long drink he turned, gave some talking passengers an angry glance and briskly trotted away back into the shrubs as quietly as he had come. Instantly, the huge animal was swallowed up by the dense bush.

At nightfall shortly after 6pm, the torches together with the vehicle's headlights came in handy. The immediate surroundings up to a few metres into the shrubs became visible. Animals that had been near the road, on our approach disappeared into the vegetation. Any creatures further away were hidden in the darkness, invisible to our eyes. The presence of the ubiquitous impala in the distance could be deduced by gatherings of many pairs of flickering lights, their eyes shining like small candles in the dark. Glittering spots a little higher up were zebras or wildebeest. We not only saw the reflection in their iris, we also heard a few sound signals between the animals which the guide explained to us.

Out of the night, two slender jackals of no more than 50cm in height turned up in the grass right by the road. They must have been driven by great curiosity. Sniffing the air, they were staring up to the people in the vehicle, their long ears pricked in astonishment. They stiffened in indignation. Offended by the insensitive noise many of the passengers made, talking and laughing, the small and charming hunters hurried away in disgust. I would have done the same had I been given the choice.

A rhino discovered by the lights, fled into the dark bushes. Either to get away from all the commotion, or, as Rudyard Kipling might have suggested, to get rid of the cake-crumbs that tickled him. I guess it was not because what someone had put inside his skin to punish his stealing the cake but because of the noise on board the vehicle.

Disruptive sounds made by guests were the last thing we expected on a game drive at night. Why these people were out here, I did not quite understand. To our disappointment, we did not see as many animals as we could have, I assume. After three hours we returned to the camp. Our own outings were more successful and enjoyable.

Shrill sounds in the morning

Fortified by early morning tea, the following day we were preparing for a drive in the microbus we had hired. Leaving the cottage to go to the car, we heard an earth-shattering sound coming from the direction of our parking spot. Horrified, we ran.

It was indeed our vehicle. Why the alarm had gone off before we had even approached let alone touched it, remained unexplained and a mystery. I am sure, guests who had chosen to ignore the alarm clock by their bedside were rudely awakened by this bone-chilling wake-up call from our minibus. Game spotters in the car park getting ready for their outing, assured us that car alarms going off unprovoked was not a rare occurrence. Receiving this piece of well meant but unsettling news, I hesitantly opened the doors, and, amazingly, the system calmed down, without offering an excuse for its bad behaviour. Cautiously I got behind the steering wheel, started the engine, and everything was fine. Irritated and embarrassed, we quickly left the camp.

Annoyed and unsettled, it took me quite a while to calm down. Gradually, the intensity of the bush and the first rays of sunshine had a soothing effect on me. Relaxing, we were hoping for inspiring animal sightings despite this inauspicious start of the day.

The rattling beginning of this outing was topped by our microbus a few days later.

Dramatis personae on a tree

Gently rolling along, we became aware of deep hollow vibrations. With the window panes lowered, we caught a strange booming sound which we had never heard before. Slowly creeping on, gradually the sound became more intense. We found its source. Near the road, we spotted some large birds against the rising morning sky. Three black hornbills were perched high up on the thick branches of a dead tree. Spellbound we listened to their lamenting and complaining. Reverberating through the silent morning air and travelling far across the trees and shrubs, the booms flooded the quiet world of dawn.

The three grey shadows on the dark wooden skeleton evoked three mythological figures, the moirai of Greek or the parcae of Roman times. They decided over human fate and destiny. Those would have been dressed in white; these, however, were not. To me, they were the three witches in William Shakespeare's *Macbeth*. They were probably just pondering "when shall we three meet again? in thunder, lightning, or in rain?" (act I, scene 1). The three sisters on the tree were just as mysterious as those in the drama. Different from the play, they did not vanish after their performance but stayed where they were. The tranquillity of the early morning, the dark silhouettes against the grey sky, together with the vibrating booms made for a spooky atmosphere and a magical moment at the same time. After quite some time we dragged ourselves away from the mystic stage up there on the tree.

Later research told us that they must have been southern ground hornbills. Had there been more light we might have seen that in fact only parts of them were black, namely their legs, feet and their straight beak. Their throat and upper neck, however, were red. Like the secretaries, they were birds which spend a good part of the day walking on the ground in search of food like fruits and insects, small reptiles or young birds.

Not long after, we discovered more hornbills. A pair of them was perched on a low branch beside the road. Their calls did not sound plaintive as did their cousins' in the dead tree but rather grating or saw-like. They probably were southern yellow-billed hornbills as their curved bills were of a distinct yellow. Otherwise they were not really colourful. They had a dark grey crown and nape, their plumage was blackish-grey and whitish-grey, their feet and legs were black. Sitting close together they might have been Romeo and Juliet, exchanging vows of love, as in Shakespeare's tragedy, "my true love's passion" (act II, scene 2). Only having eyes for each other, they took no notice of the car driving by at close range. Hopefully things worked out better for them than for the couple in Verona.

With the sun rising, the increasing light revealed the beauty and the creatures of the veld. Large and small groups of pretty impala could be seen quietly grazing but ever alert of danger. A couple of cute warthogs were running for cover not wanting to have anything to do with us. Two giraffes were browsing high up, a third was not far away from them and us. He was just standing there, ruminating and watching. Every now and then, we saw spread-out herds of zebras, a group in the distance, another family crossing the road not minding us very much as long as the vehicle did not come too close. Zebras have very sharp senses, always on their guard, reading sound, smell and sight around them, ever ready to run from danger.

We drove around the system of dirt roads with the navigator checking our progress against a detailed map of the Krugerpark. All around us was savannah-woodland. The areas we drove through offered a great variety of vegetation: dense scrub, impenetrable thickets, small trees, and stretches of open grassland. It was a soft landscape where undulating plains or low rolling hills gave way to shallow valleys.

This was the 'wonder-world of the Bushveld' as Sir Percy Fitzpatrick, in his famous book *Jock of the Bushveld* (p15), characterized the region he worked in and travelled through with his little dog in the 1880s. I am sure at some point we were driving on the very waggon route he had taken from the Lydenburg goldfields via Pretorius Kop to Delagoa Bay at the Indian Ocean through what is now the Krugerpark.

Stopped in our tracks

Our patience was severely put to the test. For the next four and a half hours we did not find any more animals, let alone some of the more exciting creatures. Not even impala. There was no game anywhere. They had all gone somewhere else. Simply vanished. But of course they were somewhere, we just did not discover them. As the day was warming up, they were looking for a shady spot and were not in the open, but behind bushes or under trees. We were on the brink of despair. Not even a piece of biltong or boerewors cheered us up. This was not going to be our day at all.

Despondent we crept on.

Coming slowly round a curve in the road, we got the most incredible surprise. A sleek cheetah was strolling along on the sand right ahead of our vehicle. I decided it was a female because she was slender and beautiful. She was not bothered in the least by our appearance, with her acute sense of smell and hearing she certainly had been aware of the vehicle's approach on the gravel road for minutes. I switched off the engine.

The animal was unconcerned by the sudden change from noise to silence. The window panes went down a bit. Now we could appreciate the sounds around us. We heard the gravel crunch gently under the cat's soft paws.

The cheetah turned and leisurely strolled towards us. The dangerous hunter could easily be taken for a friendly pet as, like a domestic cat, the fastest land animal sat down immediately in front of our vehicle.

Mesmerized, we sat and watched; we did not stir and hardly breathed. There she remained for quite a while appearing content with her life. And so were we.

Intrigued, I could not resist taking a photo. Very slowly and quietly, I lowered the window pane and slowly and quietly leaned out with the camera in my hand. I did not dare lean out more for a good shot but was happy with what was possible without irritating the animal. Better a bad picture than none at all. Undoubtedly, the park authorities would not have approved my action. Such an arresting sight, I felt however, calls for a memento.

Quietly, I closed the window again. Almost. The cat did not seem to be troubled by my movements. I am sure, with her excellent sense of hearing, the cheetah had not missed that something was going on behind her but was not concerned about it. I guess, like a film star, she was used to the effect she had on impressionable admirers.

It was an idyllic scene, perfected by a light breeze that was gently moving the leaves of the trees and shrubs.

After a while she became restless. Her tail, her head and eyes indicated that something had come up. She rose and listened intently. Ears pricked, the cat walked over to the right side of the road. From the vantage point of a termite mound, alternately, she watched us and screened the savannah for a time. Catching a telling sound or picking up a promising scent, with a meaning-business-expression on her face, the cheetah walked into the nearby tall grass and out of sight. The gentle rustling of the blades of grass giving way to her slim body was faintly perceptible, revealing where she was going.

After all, the captivating cat had made our day.

That experience again confirmed the lesson of our first morning in the Krugerpark, when William taught us not to expect anything and wait for the animals to appear at their own time.

I recalled a few lines in one of my African books. Knowing the whims of the bush, a seasoned driver and hunter gave his advice to the young and still inexperienced transport-rider Percy Fitzpatrick: "Don't go fill yourself up with tomfool notions 'bout lions and tigers waitin' behind every bush. You won't see one in a twelvemonth! Most like you won't see a buck for a week!" He could have said this to us, when we first set out watching animals. Besides plenty of patience, careful circumspection was required: "You don't know what to do, what to wear, how to walk, how to look, or what to look for; and you'll make as much noise as a traction engine." The animals' senses are far superior to those of humans, and they also know their territory far better than the hunter. He went on: "This ain't open country; it's bush; they can see and hear, and you can't. An' as for big game, you won't see any for a long while yet, so don't go fool yourself!"[21]

Appreciating the expert hunter's superior skill and long experience, we did our best to follow his guidance.

A very tall trio

Half an hour later, two handsome Greater Kudu stood among the shrubs not far away from the road. The large antelopes could be distinguished by their distinct white vertical stripes. Being hornless, they were females. Only males have a divergent set of horns that can grow up to a length of 1.5m. In spite of those long horns, their preferred habitat is bush country. Concerned about their ability to navigate

---

[21] Jock of the Bushveld, p18.

their way around the twigs and shrubbery without getting entangled in them, John Barrow, Private Secretary to the Earl of Macartney, the first British governor of the Cape colony, travelling in South Africa in the late 1790s wrote in his narrative: "The koodoo [...] its strong spiral horns are three feet in length, and seem to be very ill adapted for the convenience of the animal in the thick covert."[22] In fact, the kudu are perfectly well suited for life in thick bushlands where they feel safe. The spectacular horns might determine the winner in a competition and the fight over females.

In a patch of shrubs and trees, we saw three giraffes of the same height standing close together. Not feeling disturbed by us, they continued eating leaves and small twigs high up in a few tall acacia trees. Showing a pronounced sense of fashion, they were wearing three different coats, looking similar but not precisely the same. Just like three girlfriends who aimed at being dressed in a matching style but avoided wearing identical frocks.

Slowly driving on, Peter spotted a group of fifteen elephants making their way up a gentle valley. Moving along in a compact body they all had an air of determination about them. Every member of the herd knew their lunch time destination, which probably was Matjulu Waterhole on the far end of the valley over the hill, not very far from where we were also headed.

---

[22] An account of travels into the interior of southern Africa, I, p 105.

Sustained by our provisions and the excitement of the morning's encounters, we returned to the camp after a roundtrip of almost eight hours and 170km, only to hop into our car again soon after.

We got more than we had bargained for.

Displeasing a giant

On the brief afternoon trip we saw a number of giraffe, zebras, warthogs, kudu and a duiker. Since it was mid afternoon and therefore still a little too warm, it was too early for most animals to be out and about. Avoiding the heat, they remained in the shade under their parasols of trees and shrubs, sleeping and bonding.

The only animal that was not resting was a giant. Heading back to camp and coming round a bend, we came up to a huge elephant bull walking near the gravel road. We were surprised and rather startled. I slowed down the car to a crawl. His determined steps indicated a certain purpose. His enormous size was terrifying, making the vehicle look like a toy. I stopped to stay further back, with white knuckles I held on to the wheel. It was not far enough for his liking. Slowing down his pace, the elephant looked at us, not liking our presence. We held our breath. Then he walked on, shaking his head in disapproval. Besides this gesture of displeasure, he did not do anything threatening. But he glanced at the car in no uncertain terms. Did he contemplate tossing the trespasser? My pulse quickened. While he was gradually turning to the right away from the road, giving him a wide berth, we crept on in the grass on the opposite side of the road keeping our distance to him. I was glad when he disappeared into the shrubs.

We moved on with a deep sigh of relief, but were not truly convinced to be out of harm's way. We were somewhat unsettled by the encounter. In particular me, the one behind the wheel.

Anxiously scanning the shrubs to our right, I drove on with mixed feelings. We vaguely suspected it was not the last we had seen of the elephant bull. We developed ideas where he might go, one of which was the waterhole, dismissing that as being too far, but not being entirely certain. After several kilometres I turned right towards Matjulu to see if there were any animals, as the place was a well-visited spot for a gulp of fresh water.

Feeling slightly uneasy, I parked in a corner near the trees with the engine running, just in case. There were one or two other cars waiting for thirsty animals to come for a drink but none had arrived. After only a few minutes one appeared. Having taken a short cut through the trees and shrubs, it was indeed the very elephant bull we had escaped from. He came walking over the hill at a pretty fast pace and headed for the water. He is seeking me out I thought, remorsefully. Which he surely didn't, only wanting to fill his trunk with water and squirt it into his mouth. Seeing him rapidly coming towards the place, we did not linger another moment. With a second sigh of relief we made a speedy exit from his territory and dashed to the camp for cover.

With the help of a steadying pint of sweet juice, I recovered my spirits.

After the scary experience in the wilderness, I was glad to attend the conference and listen to talks and presentations. The ensuing discussions were perfectly suited to disperse any thoughts about elephants.

But not for long, because in the evening it was animals again.

The Kruger rangers' challenges

A wildlife talk had been arranged for the conference. A ranger in his smart uniform welcomed us to his presentation. If I recall correctly, he was the section ranger responsible for the region around Berg-en-Dal. Rangers in such a position have many duties: supervising and inspecting their area, monitoring the game in their district, checking for diseases, devising anti-poaching policies and apprehending poachers, investigating reports of dead animals or attacks on humans, removing animals from rest camps, as well as communicating with visitors, naming but a few of their varied tasks. Rangers also have to provide leadership, and enforce the law and fire regulations.

The Kruger National Park is divided into a number of units headed by a section ranger. Some stations are located in central areas, others in less accessible regions and even quite isolated spots, as in the early years of the park. Unlike in the beginnings, today many rangers are married and often their wives and children are also living inside the Krugerpark.

How unpredictable and dangerous but also exciting and rewarding life on a far away station can be is told in *The Wilderness Family*. The author Kobie Kruger is the wife of a game ranger of the park and mother of three daughters. Written from a family point of view, she describes their daily encounters with the wild creatures on their isolated station and their shock and ordeal when finally transferred back to civilization. The book gives an insight into the continuous and never ending challenges faced by the human and animal population of the park. It details the diverse responsibilities, frustrating setbacks, thrilling encounters, mortal dangers and various accidents of her husband during their seventeen-year tenure on different ranger stations.

The ranger's lecture covered plants and animals in the park. With over 2,000 different plant species the botanic diversity of flowers, trees and grasses is noteworthy. Plants are ranging from aloes to orchids, from marula trees to mopane and baobab with a significant number of different types of grasses. There are also a great variety of fish like mudfish and carps, reptiles like lizards, snakes and crocodiles, and birds like eagles, orioles and parrots.

When it came to mammals the ranger spoke not only about numbers, but also about culling and poaching.

Managing the numbers

We were given a recent count of animals in the Krugerpark: as far as my notes say, at the time, there were 22,000 buffalos and 9,000 elephants; 3,000 white rhinos and 300 black rhinos; 1,500 leopards, 250 cheetahs, 2,000 lions and 2,000 hyenas. Whichever the numbers at the time, we considered ourselves lucky to encounter some species more than once. According to the figures published on the website of South African National Parks, the estimates for the financial year 2010/2011 were (a recent census could not be found): buffalos 37,130, elephants 13,750, leopards 1,000, wildebeest between 6,400 and 13,100, lions around 1,700, hyenas just over 5,000 and cheetahs 120. Comparing the figures makes plain how the numbers of animals and their distribution in the park are affected by environmental aspects or meteorological factors. But also by human interference.

Surveys of the game population had been done since the 1960s. Aircraft have become indispensable in establishing the number of animals since the 1970s. The annual census is a management tool giving estimates on actual numbers, information on distribution patterns and habitat occupation. A comparison of previous and later polls suggests that animal numbers vary with annual cycles and general weather conditions. Temperature, droughts, cyclones, bush fires as well as precipitation and floods are parameters included in the assessment. The documented data are mapped and evaluated providing material for analysis and statistics. As Kruger National Park is also a research area, the results reveal insights and offer conclusions for management strategies as well as future resources and funding programs.

The monitoring of animals is also used for culling activities. The operation aimed at reducing the amount of certain animals, a process that at times was deemed necessary to manage the park and control its game. For example between 1967 and 1996 about 13,000 elephants were killed. Bruce Bryden as Chief Ranger, Instructor and Head of Conservation Support Services in the Kruger National Park until 2001 directed many of the culls. He explains the procedures in the first part of chapter four in his book *A Game Ranger Remembers*. Even though the methods may have been modified, killing of animals on a reserve is still controversial.

Dealing with poaching

The ranger's talk also addressed the very serious and persistent problem of poaching. In 2013 alone, a staggering 1,000 white and black rhinos have been killed in South Africa, nearly all of them in Krugerpark. In 2016 about 460 rhinos have been found dead, in 2020 it was still more than 240. Over the last few years, the Kruger Park Rangers have been assisted in their anti-poaching efforts by the Hemmersbach Rhino Force, a dedicated private conservation initiative by the global IT company based in Germany, that uses military grade equipment and the latest surveillance technology. Thanks to their state-of-the-art tools and training, they are able to operate at night thus preventing at least some of the slaughter. But the fight is ongoing.

Rhinos had been on the brink of total annihilation before. White rhinos had been hunted in the region to near extinction by 1890. In the 1960s, in a relocation program they were reintroduced over a twelve year period. Black rhinos were reintroduced in the 1970s after having been eradicated by 1936.

Trade in rhino horn for the alleged benefit of human health still results in large numbers of dead rhinos in Africa. Despite dehorning or translocating the animals, temporary bans, attempts to make the trade illegal, conferences and resolutions, as well as a wide range of efforts to stop the poaching, the operations are still continuing. Via Mozambique, the horns of those rhinos are exported mainly to Asia to be made into traditional medicine as treatment for gout and rheumatism, even though pharmaceutical properties have not been proven. They are also valued as aphrodisiac or made into objects as status symbols. With high demand and soaring prices, incentives for poachers are considerable, and profits for sellers are well worth their while. In an attempt to counteract the devastating hunts, biologists in Britain have developed a method to manufacture horns that look the same as the real ones. Whether this will help the survival of the critically threatened animals remains to be seen.

At the time when the Sabi Game Reserve and, indeed, the Kruger National Park were established, there were just a few dozen elephants that were rarely seen by the rangers. They moved, or rather fled, into the region in greater numbers only in the 1950s when they were hunted in neighbouring Mozambique on a large scale. Slaughtered for their tusks, since the 1980s elephants have been killed in ever increasing numbers on the African continent. While tens of thousands have been shot in recent years in Africa (in Tanzania, within less than 40 years, the number of elephants has been reduced to just over 50,000 down from 316,000 in the late 1970s), in Kruger the numbers are lower than those for rhinos, with not many shot since 2004. But in 2015 poachers killed 19 animals, in 2017 the number rose to 30, in 2020 it went down to 16 tuskers. Conventions on the subject, the occasional ivory ban in some countries (e.g. China in December 2017), or a public burning of poached ivory in Kenya in 1989 (12 tonnes) and in 2016 (105 tonnes), in 2012 in Gabon, in 2015 in Mozambique, did not change much.

Rhinos or elephants, or indeed any animals, do not stand a chance against assault rifles, wire snares or poisoned fruit. Killing those animals has grown into big business and involves crime networks operating worldwide. The poachers can be bushmeat traders or horn and ivory poachers working on contract. They are heavily armed and highly organised professionals. Raids are meticulously planned, and their tactics are becoming ever more cunning. During encounters with them the rangers of Krugerpark are often putting their lives in danger when being out-manoeuvred and out-numbered by the criminals.

Out on patrol

Besides the rangers there are the game guards who are looking after the animals and the land. Usually they are locals with in-depth bush knowledge and first-rate tracking skills. They know how to detect pugmarks and droppings of animals and to interpret their spoors, but also those of the poachers. Most of them are trained in armed combat and are experts in movement techniques and tactics. Their job involves checking on the well-being of game, observing herd sizes, reporting on animal numbers and distribution, controlling water points; however, gathering intelligence, tracking down and arresting poachers has become an ever more important part of their tasks in recent years.

On two different roads in the park, we had seen teams of two armed field rangers out on monitoring and policing duty. They were not in cars but on bicycles. Presumably the idea was, when spotting illegal activities on their silent patrol, to radio back to base and raise the alarm. On two wheels they would not be heard, but would hardly be able to escape fast enough. Even though cars might betray their presence, on four wheels they could quickly get away from danger. Considering the extent and brutality of poaching, it is hard to believe that a bicycle unit of two was supposed to fight anyone. While armed with rifles, those rangers out in the field looked under-equipped without any other means of defence against attacks either from humans or from animals, from tusks or from gun barrels. But then, I am sure, at Krugerpark they all know what they are doing, which might not be too obvious to a visitor.

Poaching is nothing new

In the starting phase of the Krugerpark, poaching had already been an issue. The first warden, Major James Stevenson-Hamilton, right from taking up his post in 1902 did his best to establish a no-shooting rule to stop the reduction of wildlife. He and his staff had to fight on several fronts: the white hunters and the local tribes. While farmers or passing Boer groups used their rifles to great effect, the native hunters for a time mainly used bows and arrows, wire snares as well as a variety of traps and in due time turned to other weapons. "Trouble with white poachers has been rare, and of a minor kind, but almost ever since the reserve was proclaimed, it has been subject along all its borders to encroachment by native hunters, sometimes appearing in large bands and provided with firearms." [23]

Poachers were resourceful when it came to disguising their tracks. Game Ranger Sergeant Harry Wolhuter knew all about their tricks: "The poaching fraternity became increasingly bold and venturesome, penetrating a good deal further into the park than they were wont to do previously." They contrived particular methods of deception: "These poachers had to cross at least two fairly wide motor roads and in traversing these they would adopt the plan of walking backwards - taking care to leave a well-defined spoor on the road with the object of misleading any of my native rangers who might locate the spoor."

The poachers did not hesitate to turn their weapons on the rangers. Wolhuter himself on occasion became the target when surprising a poacher in his hiding place: "He was quite unaware of our presence until he reached the camp and had observed me and my horse and then, in a flash, he withdrew his rifle from his shoulder, pointed it straight at me, and fired. Fortunately for myself, and no doubt greatly to his surprise, he missed me, and turning about he made a rush for the spruit." [24] When firing in return, to the ranger's shock, his gun malfunctioned and the poacher escaped.

The more recent battle against poaching in Kruger National Park is graphically described in chapter seven in *A Game Ranger Remembers*. The poachers whom Chief Ranger Bryden had to face were highly trained ex-soldiers with an impressive arsenal of weaponry. Even when the poachers were caught, however, it was not necessarily a success. At one time, to his utter consternation, he had

---

[23] South African Eden, p263.
[24] Memories of a game ranger, p146, 152.

to release a group of them for political reasons after it was found that the prisoners were high ranking officials from neighbouring Mozambique.

Then and now, poaching has subsided for a time, only to emerge with a vengeance. Often rangers, and certainly animals, were and are no match for the killers. Usually anti-poaching units are vastly out-gunned by ruthless well-armed commandos operating for African syndicates and international cartels, that not only traffic in animal parts but also in narcotics. If arrests are made, it is mainly men who are desperately poor and not the big bosses who are behind the organisations.

How high the obstacles are to catch the real criminals and how politics, law enforcement, bureaucracy, corruption and big money are involved, can also be seen in Kenya. The numerous initiatives by Richard Leakey, FRS, professor of anthropology, many years director of the Kenyan Wildlife Service, as described in detail in his book *Wildlife Wars*, demonstrate the perils, controversies, and the futility of anti-poaching efforts in general.

Everywhere in Africa, the battle for horns, tusks and skins shows little signs of abating.

Trophy hunting

While the illegal slaying of animals by the poaching gangs is a lucrative commercial enterprise, the legal killing of animals for fun against large sums of money is also big business. Today, in certain circles it is still practiced as it was more than hundred years ago. With the onset of white big-game hunting for pleasure at the end of the 19th century, hunters were after their prey as a return for their expensive efforts, hoping for vain glory.

Amongst the most sought-after prizes was always the biggest cat, considered the highest accolade: "The shooting of a lion, fair and square, and face to face, was the Blue Riband of the Bush." A dead majestic creature at one's feet as a self-congratulatory trophy to gratify one's vanity. In the 1880, the transport-riders of the goldfields had amongst their loads what was left of once magnificent animals: "Trophies, carried back with pride or by force of habit, lay scattered about, neglected and forgotten. [...] How many a 'record' head must have gone then, when none had thought of time or means to save them! Horns and skins lay in jumbled heaps in the yards or sheds of the big trading stores."[25] Lions, buffalo or rhinos were not only killed but left to waste and decay in a dark corner.

More wild encounters

One lovely morning we were cruising through a beautiful stretch of savannah. The sun was up but dawn had not yet quite retreated. We lowered the window panes a little more than ten centimetres. A breeze of cool air floated into the car. It was very quiet, a few soft sounds from far away and hardly perceptible reached our ears.

All of a sudden, a massive rhino emerged from the bushes on our right. Amazingly, we had not heard or seen a thing, considering the bulk and size of the animal. Fitting the mood of the moment, he seemed to be on a relaxed morning stroll. Not looking left or right at all, he walked slowly across the reddish dirt road without bothering about us at all. Whether he had noticed the vehicle was hard to tell but probable. A rhino's sense of smell and sound is far better than his eyesight which is very poor.

---

[25] Jock of the Bushveld, p20, 14-15.

'Where are you coming from, we have not heard you breaking through the scrub.'

'I didn't mean to surprise you, I caught a whiff of your polluting emissions from 20m away and had to investigate.'

'Our apologies for offending your olfactory system, but that is what cars do.'

'I know, and I also know that your visit helps to support the park and us animals. But still, I don't like those clouds of fumes wafting through the greenery.'

'Next time, we will be on horseback then, hoping that is an acceptable compromise. Bye for now.'

This was a huge animal that resembled the description of the naturalist William John Burchell, when he came across one such specimen in 1811: "The first view of this beast, suggested the idea of an enormous hog, to which [...] it bears some outward resemblance [...] but in its shapeless clumsy legs and feet, it more resembles the hippopotamus and elephant."[26] This one did not display any clumsiness but trotted on in a well thought-through and balanced manner. As silently as the rhino had emerged he disappeared into the scrub. Despite his size he melted away instantly.

We spent quite a long time in the company of two young hyenas. Resting on the kerbside in the warm sunshine, the lovely youngsters' faces were very cute. Taking a brief sleepy look at us, the siblings were convinced we were not posing any danger and resumed snoozing. Their little ears, however, kept scanning their surroundings. They were not bothered or worried in the least by the white vehicle. We did not see any adult hyena nearby, but I am sure there was one watching over them. All four of us enjoyed the tranquil morning. After half an hour another car spoiled our idyll, and we parted company.

---

[26]Travels in the interior of southern Africa, II, p75.

Driving on, we came across two other youngsters of a different species, but they were not on their own. In an area of trees, shrubs and green grass, a family of waterbucks was following our movements. Their coats were of a warm brownish colour with a very white circular line around the root of their tails. The mother waterbuck with her two pretty youngsters did not appear too worried about the car even though we were not more than three metres away. She gazed at us from a sunny spot under a tall tree before wandering off with her offspring.

At Biyamiti Dam two monitor lizards were basking on the rocks to warm up in the sunshine. Fast runners and excellent swimmers, they had chosen an appropriate patch from where to hunt on land and in water. They were after carrion or just any unfortunate creature that happened to come their way. While we were driving by they had no such intentions.

The water also attracted many birds. Perched on high branches above the dam, brightly coloured kingfisher prepared to spear unsuspecting fish. Darting through the lake's surface, they pinned their victim and swiftly retrieved their prize. Not far away, on his vantage point, a fish eagle was also on the lookout before swooping down and snatching a fish with his clawed talons.

Pandemonium

We drove along a lonely side road through open bushland without having seen another car for a long time. There were some patches of shrub but not many trees except a very tall specimen not far from the road. As we rolled nearer to it, we realized that it was a busy place.

It had been seized by a large group of boisterous vervet monkeys. In bursts of hysterical passions, they chattered non-stop and restlessly jumped through the branches. In the middle of the road, I switched off the engine to hear them communicate. They stopped and watched, their black faces scrutinizing us with intense curiosity. We did not look or smell like their usual predators. They started discussing that strange item sitting there on the road without moving. Various opinions were offered and not agreed upon. Not finding an answer to their satisfaction, they continued what had been interrupted. Making a tremendous din, they were chasing each other on the ground, rushing up the tree, leaping from one branch to the next, or just dashing about. After a while we decided that we had seen and heard enough of their antics and screams.

We were ready to move on, but the vehicle was not. I turned the ignition key, the engine did not respond. Instead, the car alarm started to go off every few seconds. For unknown reasons, the anti-theft-device had become activated. The system was constantly emitting ear-splitting frantic tones, drowning the peaceful area in aggressive noise.

To our and the poor monkeys' dismay the high-volume alarm did not cease blaring.

Most likely, the monkeys had never in their lives heard such blood-chilling sounds. Stunned and startled, they stared from their perch with wide eyes. They stiffened in horror, their electric activity stopped sharply. With high-pitched shrieks and screaming with fright, they jumped to the ground. With long loping bounds they fled the infernal scene in great terror and left us to our fate.

Consulting the handbook did not help; it did not give any instructions what to do in the situation we found ourselves in, as an alarm system was not even mentioned. We tried a few things, without any success. There was a phone number given, but our mobile did not work here. With the incessant piercing blare shattering my nerves more and more, I got very angry with the rental company. That did not help much. With the air-conditioning not on, the vehicle was hotting up. And so was my temper. I imagined being stuck here for the rest of the day and into the night. I entertained nervous thoughts of the vehicle being tossed about by a confused rhino, stampeded into pulp by a mob of buffalos, or besieged by a pride of lions ready to pounce through the roof. They certainly would have more sinister motives than Winnie-the-Pooh's ever enthusiastic bouncing and pouncing friend Tigger. Ideas of that kind clearly were not uplifting. While I was becoming exasperated and furious, Peter, always more reasonable and collected, remained composed, but rather worried all the same.

Our only hope was another car coming along this remote track in the wilderness. Though an official road, our chances seemed very slim indeed. I nearly despaired, considering where we were.

After a nerve-wrecking time of about one hour, a car appeared indeed in the distance. Slowly and hesitatingly it moved towards us, unsure what to expect. After all, we were in the land of kidnapping, robbery and murder. Cautiously, it came to a halt 20m away.

There were four people in the car. We waved to them and signalled with the manual, pressing it against the front windscreen. While our vehicle continued emitting that awful noise, they understood that we had some kind of a problem. Identifying us as foreigners and excluding any malicious intent on our part, their car came closer and stopped in front of ours.

Against the rules of the park, I got out. With such a hell of a noise any animals would have run as fast as possible, so there was not much danger. The driver of the other car then did the same. He had been wondering why there was a vehicle right in the middle of the road without any sign of giving way. Having heard the high-pitched alarm and zooming in on it while approaching, he had suspected something might be wrong. He was a South African with a mobile phone. Ringing the emergency number at Avis did not help at all, the person answering did not have a clue. Appalled by such incompetence, we were then waiting for his son, a mechanic, following in his own car somewhere behind. After another wait, he turned up. The expert was familiar with temperamental vehicles and knew how to deal with the undocumented feature. Within a second the alarm was off, and the engine restarted.

I did not want to think about what might have happened had no one turned up. Ever. We hoped the monkeys had recovered from their shock and returned to their tree. Not looking right or left for any more animals, we took the shortest route back to base.

After a shower and a drink, I was still angry with that useless rental company. The supposed purpose of the immobilizer was to prevent the unauthorized use of a vehicle, but not to prevent the fully authorized one. Peter's dry comment was 'security by obscurity'.

A bar of chocolate helped to recalibrate ourselves after that ordeal.

Kipling's notorious elephant youngster

A few hours later we had recovered and, unfazed, drove out again in the afternoon. A kudu family was walking on the tarmac road but disappeared into the bush when we got closer. A few impala were gathered in the distance, they looked up but were not bothered at all. We saw a group of zebras braying madly and running into a thicket. A few majestic giraffes not far from the road were chewing away in the sky, not taking any notice.

A herd of elephants had congregated around a huge water tank. We counted thirteen adults and three youngsters in the group. With plenty of water and an abundance of grass, this spot was obviously a vital place for the animals. The adults understood the importance of the patch, the calves were not concerned with anything serious.

With the infants playing and doing nothing but mischief, I thought one of them might be Rudyard Kipling's ever demanding elephant's child possessed of 'satiable curtiosity' [sic], whose tiresome inquisitiveness is pestering his extended family till, at their wits end, they resort to a measured amount of violence. That still does not deter the little elephant from carrying on his annoying methods of finding out. I did not hear whether the little chap we were watching still asked too many questions and got spanked for it, or, whether he already was in the stage of spanking back. Probably neither, since all of them were relaxed and did not discuss what the crocodile has for dinner.

Instead, some of the adult elephants consumed their green food with a watchful eye on the youngsters, while others lifted their long trunks over the rim of the tank to take a thirst-quenching gulp. They did not spank anyone.

The family did not show any intention of going anywhere soon, not even to the grey-green, greasy Limpopo River. Nor were we inclined to go that far.

Death lurking in the greenery

We were already on our way back to the camp and just crossing a bridge, when suddenly, with much excitement in his voice, Peter shouted: 'Stop, stop the car'. I slammed on the brakes, and the vehicle skidded to a halt with an abrupt jerk in the middle of the bridge.

He had spotted a large herd of about a hundred buffalos. They were grazing away contently in the lush green river bed right below us on our right. They took advantage of the abundance of juicy grass, slowly munching their way through the rich supply. With the window panes down we heard their grunts from our lofty vantage point. Without a care in the world they were only focussed on the plentiful green blades.

The buffalos were blissfully ignorant of what might happen in a little while. A fatal mistake.

Predators were closing in on them, and they were totally unaware of them. One was approaching to the rear of the group. To the left of the bridge, behind the herd, Peter discovered a lioness crouching in the tall grass. Slowly and carefully she was inching her way forward stealthily, watching and assessing the buffalos intently. Her eyes and ears were fixed to select her prey. She was probably looking for a young, sick, old or wounded animal knowing perfectly well that a healthy target was dangerous. She seemed to be on her own but most probably was not.

As it takes more than one lion to go after a buffalo, there were certainly more around remaining out of sight. At this stage of the hunt, the pride did their best to stay hidden in the shrubs close by. As long as the powerful buffalos stay tightly together, they are able to fend off the attackers. An animal separated from the herd does not stand much of a chance against several of the cats. Whether one was already singled out we did not make out. Quietly stalking their prey, they intended to get close to their target in order to make the charge from a short distance.

Whether the lions' strategy worked out this time, we could not find out. Unfortunately we were not able to watch any drama unfolding below since the camp gates were due to close shortly. We had to hurry back to base. With a thank you and sorry nod we slipped into the compound more than five minutes late without being reprimanded by the lenient guard.

A rare black rhino and warthog families

The next morning found us on the road to Lower Sabie. For quite some time no animals were to be seen or heard. Nothing much was happening. We enjoyed our slow drive through the bushveld.

In an area littered with boulders and bushes, Peter slowed down the chauffeur. Being good at spotting, he noticed some movement about 15m from the road behind a rock among shrubs in the thicket. Almost undistinguishable from its surroundings there was a rhino. A closer look with our field glasses suggested that, its upper lip appearing prolonged, this was a black rhino. Rather secretive and rarely seen, this one was the only one we saw; the other 299 living in the park eluded us. He was shyer than the white rhinos we had encountered so far and kept his distance. Moving among the shrubs back and forth, he looked in our direction and apparently thought hard, what the meaning of sound and smell might be which filled the air so unbecomingly. He turned the matter over in his mind, weighing up the pros and cons. Arriving at a decision, the rhino did not wish to find out more and walked further away into the bushes and out of sight.

Travelling on side road S82 we passed through warthog country. The flat and open stretch of land offered them a lot of grass to eat and nutritious bulbs and roots to dig up. Without a coat to speak of but a thin mane along the neck to the middle of the back and with two pairs of upwards curving tusks, they were not attractive. Although not the sweetest looking creatures, they had an appealing charm. They even looked cute in their special way, in particular the piglets. Small family groups were busy foraging in the dust, so the car advanced very slowly along the dirt road not too far from where they were at work. After eyeing us for a while, they grew uneasy. The mothers motioned their numerous offspring to stay close. Glancing with suspicion at the alien object that was crawling through their territory, they all hurried away behind clusters of grass with their tails held proudly upright.

We parked at Mpondo Lake, near Lower Sabie Camp, located on the eastern side of Krugerpark and 11km from the Mozambique border. I positioned the car in such a way as to give us front row seats.

Bushes and trees behind the flat uncovered shore on the far side gave the animals enough protection to check for danger prior to walking out into the open and to the lake. A warthog family of eight were taking a stroll along the shore, wisely they did not walk to the water's edge. The youngsters were called back as soon as they began straying. The mother was well aware of who was in the lake.

The log floating in the water was reason enough for being cautious; it was indeed the resident croc as our binoculars revealed. Imitating a piece of wood adrift in the lake was not difficult for the reptile and seems to be rather a matter of habit, given how easily one can at first glance take such an animal for a stranded piece of trunk.

When you are Kipling's young elephant out on a mission, you do not recognize a crocodile for a crocodile, particularly not when it is winking two eyes at you. Instead, you address it ever so politely, only wishing to find out about the crocodile's plan for a meal and finding the answer by being pulled into the water. There is not always a bi-coloured rock python to intervene. But when you are a smart warthog, you cannot so easily be deceived.

A hippo going walkabout

The only other creature in the water was a huge hippo having a good time and staying submerged most of the time. The giant was less to the liking of the reptile than the antelopes or little warthogs of the area. In fact, the hippo was the ruler of the pond, and the croc was well advised to stay away from him. It has often been documented that hippos attack and kill crocodiles.

Semi-aquatic like the crocodiles, hippos have to leave the water to search for food. Mainly at dusk, but occasionally during the day. And they do not expect to meet humans on their wanderings. If they do, it usually ends up badly for man.

We saw hippos at close range on a few occasions, but never became personal with them. However, Prince William of Sweden did during his excursions in Kenya and Central Africa in 1921 with the Swedish Zoological Expedition.

He had a lovely encounter with a friendly hippo near the shore of a lake. "Like a great pig or a tightly packed sausage skin on four legs he came towards me peacefully, munching grass which was still hanging out in long ribbons from his broad, gaping jaws. It was quite a pity to disturb him, and as I had already shot one the previous day I did not want to do him any harm." They met on a track through luxuriant greenery and discussed the situation amicably: "But the path was very narrow and we were approaching each other from opposite directions. Neither he nor I wanted to step aside into the stinging nettles. Then I asked him politely in Swedish to give way. He grunted something in answer that I did not understand and screwed up his kindly little pigs' eyes meaningly. But nevertheless he came stalking straight up to me. Only a few yards separated us." A shot fired into the ground did not alter the fact that the son of the Swedish king was getting the short straw: "Yet turn he would not, however, but rushed on instead, scared out of his wits, and so close to me that I could easily have put my hand on his round back. And the one who quickly and surely ended up in the nettles was myself."[27] Having convincingly established his right of way, the huge animal dismissed his royal opponent with nonchalance.

While the prince was suffering from itching and burning, the victorious hippo continued on his interrupted bushwalk in the best of moods, quite pleased how he had extricated himself from a tight spot, I should imagine.

A nasty shock

Showing excellent manners even during a stroll in the wilderness of Africa is admirable, but when out in the bush other qualities and considerations are more of the essence. Facing a hippo or a croc demands quick thinking and presence of mind, even the rifle in your hand might not be put to adequate use. While crocodiles, when in the water, are mostly taken for a log they also come in other guises, as narrated in one of the tales in *Jock of the Bushveld*.

Hunting for guineafowl, a transport-rider experienced a very special moment: "Stepping bare-footed from rock to rock where the reeds were thin, he made no noise at all." Making no sound, the birds could not hear him, and he, while knowing where they were, could not see them well within the vegetation. He had to find another method around the problem: "The only chance of getting a shot at them was to mount one of the big rocks from which he could see down into the reeds; and he worked his way along a mud-bank towards one. A couple more steps from the mud-bank on to a low black rock would take him to the

---

[27] Among Pygmies and gorillas, p102-103.

big one." Focussing on his prey, he was not aware of the true nature of the rock until it revealed itself: "Without taking his eyes off the reeds where the guinea-fowl [sic] were he stepped cautiously on to the low black rock, and in an instant was swept off his feet, tossed and tumbled over and over, into the mud and reeds. He had stepped on the back of a sleeping crocodile; no doubt it was every bit as frightened as he was."[28] Both took to flight in opposite directions, recovering from the terrifying collision.

No such frightful surprises occurred at Mpondo Lake while we were visiting. The massive hippo stayed in the water, and so did the crocodile. Meanwhile, a group of waterbucks had arrived and was grazing right in front of our car in the company of three herons. They were all keeping an eye on the water and did not mind us at all. Not bothered by the vehicle, they knew perfectly well where danger could come from.

Since the sun was high, no more animals were coming out of the bush. But, to our surprise and delight, some were coming out of the nearby river.

A herd in the reeds

Shortly afterwards, driving along the main tarmac road, we found many cars parked on the right side of the road. Everybody was staring down onto the wide riverbed of the Sabie. What were they looking at, we were wondering, there was nothing to see. It was all greenery and nothing else. Or was it?

Apparently, there was something exciting to see. But what it was we did not realize at first. We saw nothing but vegetation. But where was the water?

---

[28] Jock of the Bushveld, p103-104.

Although the Sabie was supposed to be a perennial river we could not see flowing water. Almost all of the riverbed was covered with tall and impenetrable reeds that reached up to either bank. Besides droughts or floods, projects like afforestation, irrigation and other agricultural activities are resulting in changing land use in the catchment areas of the Sabie and other rivers. The impact of such schemes is reducing the water flow and the water balance, with some rivers changing from perennial to seasonal. The declining trend is affecting the riparian ecosystem and the cyclic water supply, which might explain why we did not see any water as the water level seemed to be low.

What we saw was not a proper riverbed but an expanse of reedbeds. Reed grasses are tall and thin plants found in wetland conditions. They form a dense system of rhizomes with roots reaching far down into the wet soil, reason why the reeds can cope with a water table even below the surface. That makes them the dominant vegetation in a river without a constant water flow.

The deep-rooted reed grasses are stabilizing the sand bars that have accumulated over time. They also offer a riverine habitat and cover for birds, they also provide food for large animals.

Then we saw the reason why all those cars were sitting there.

The abundant area of pale green vegetation was dotted with grey enormous animals pushing through the lush greenery. A large herd of elephants was slowly crossing the muddy riverbed diagonally from the bank on the far side to a particular point on ours farther ahead. How many there were was impossible to determine, since many reeds were swaying without a grey back to be seen, suggesting there were teenagers and youngsters tunnelling through the tall stems.

After the last one disappeared from sight we moved further along the road and came to another abrupt standstill. The very herd was just coming up from the river on the right and crossing over the road into the woodlands on the left of the road. It was a family of more than a dozen animals of all sizes and ages. They stayed close behind each other carefully keeping their youngsters between them. One or two of the infants seemed to show an interest in the objects on the road but were shuffled back into the line of protecting feet. Without any haste, the herd made their way into the safety of the bush.

By then, more cars had arrived and were sitting right across both lanes both ways. Watching the spectacle of the giants passing straight in front of their bonnet, everybody was thrilled by the sight. And so were we. Happy with seeing the elephants so close-up, we drove on.

All of a sudden, crossing in front of the vehicle, a large antelope came dashing headlong out of the dense shrub. The kudu was as much surprised by the car as we were about his appearing from nowhere. Both sides looked startled. Just a minute ago, we had scanned the very shrubs without spotting anything worth spotting. Materializing out of the bush, the kudu was yet another example of the perfect camouflage of animals. Just as Sir Percy Fitzpatrick came to the conclusion: "As for not seeing things, the answer is that the bush does not allow you to see much."[29]

The area chosen for the day's exploration and animal spotting had rewarded us nicely for our efforts, and we turned back to camp. While Peter dutifully went to the talks and discussions, I ambled around the camp and ended up at the viewing platform.

---

[29] Jock of the Bushveld, p142.

Put in my place by a monkey

I took a seat on the bench, renewing my acquaintance with the residents of the dam, but not intending to open another line of communication, let alone fishing for a reprimand. Which is exactly what I got.

As on the previous occasion, on the opposite bank, there were a few terrapins enjoying the warmth. The crocs were basking in the sun. These ancient creatures looked innocent and atrocious at the same time. Not blinking, they certainly did not miss anything. If they knew what happened to many of their species, they would not rest on the sand quite so unconcernedly.

While I was watching them, I was wondering why they should be turned into handbags. Making sure they always have a sufficient supply of leather, famous fashion houses raise their own crocodiles on large farms. Their products are selling at exorbitant prices, pronouncing the financial status of the owners. There are also Nile crocodile farms in South Africa, with thousands of the animals kept and killed for their skins and their meat. The country is among the largest exporters in the market.

One of my books sprang to mind, *Crocodile Fever*. It tells the story of success and failure of a crocodile hunter on the Zambesi. He shot hundreds for a living, twenty-three in one night alone. Starting at the age of eight, it became a lifelong passion. While admiring them greatly, he killed them for their skin. I could not understand why anyone would shoot animals for money, not to mention as a trophy.

Over there across the water, it was quiet and relaxed, everyone was dozing in the afternoon sunshine. But not on my side of the reservoir.

Above my head things were in full swing. From their perch high up and far from the resting reptiles, monkeys were rushing around the trees and noisily talking to each other. What they gossiped or quarrelled about, I did not understand. Peering inquisitively through the leaves, they watched me at first with great curiosity. Soon, they lost interest as I was doing nothing that could hold their attention. I was quietly sitting and observing, and that was too boring for them. I thought how confident and sure of themselves they were, recklessly racing from one branch to another, seemingly without any fears of falling into the water. It would take a croc one second to reach them.

Their seeming foolishness was hard to watch, and I could not hold back. A lucid exchange made clear who was the fool.

'Hey, are you crazy, jumping around like that', I dared.

'And who are you to tell me', one of them inquired sharply, gazing down at me with a stare.

'You could easily end up in the croc's mouth!'

'You think you are a wise one, don't you', in a scathing tone of voice, arching an ironic left eyebrow.

'Isn't it dangerous what you are doing up there?'

'What do you know!' was the contemptuous reply.

And there I was. The little chap only shrugged, his mates did the same. Hurrying along the branches, they dislodged leaves and twigs that fell onto the water's surface with a splash, accentuating their opinion about me. I heard a laugh and a chuckle from above.

The big croc swished his strong tail several times offering a knowing grin, the terrapins turned their heads to the side suppressing a faint amused smile. The birds had listened to the dialogue on a tree behind me and now twittered excitedly among themselves; such a conversation they had not heard before on the small lake.

The artful oratory and the lofty theatrics that have been played out twice for my benefit at Matjulu Dam I considered worthy a performance on a London stage.

Impala for dinner

There is no conference without a conference dinner. This one was no exception. Fitting the unique location, the evening's gathering took place outdoors.

The spacious patio adjoining the Berg-en-Dal function rooms was the perfect site. Overlooking the small Matjulu Dam and its river, we could have watched the crocs, terrapins and monkeys we had observed during the day. But it was too dark to see them. Occasionally, we only heard sounds coming from the monkeys preparing for the night. Punctuating the darkness, at times a hyena or even a lion could be heard just outside the perimeter fence. Truly, a dinner in the wilderness.

When the guests were invited to take their place and the lids of the buffet came off, I was taken aback when I learned that it was impala which was turning on the large grill. The idea that such a graceful antelope was destined to end up in my stomach was quite disgusting to me. The irritation subsided, when I accepted the fact that antelopes were eaten in South Africa just as deer in the Northern Hemisphere or kangaroo in Australia.

There were plenty of tasty dishes to choose from and a selection of African wines to go with the delicacies. Long tables promoted the renewal of friendships and the exchange of adventures in the wild as well as discussions on the conference topics and on long-distance travel.

Officially closing the evening, William as the organising chair thanked the kitchen staff for their great job in a praising speech. They, in return, thanked him for his cooperation and serenaded him with a local song. Their vocal and culinary performance earned them a lot of applause from everyone.

With a full moon and a starlit sky the evening became very cold as the night progressed. Wrapped up in blankets from our cottage, however, dinner in the bushveld under the stars in such a spectacular place made you ignore any freezing temperatures. The sounds emerging from the invisible activities in the bush close-by emphasized the fact that this was not an ordinary dinner occasion but a highly unusual and exciting setting for an evening meal. It was the magic of the bushveld.

By midnight, everybody was ready to retire. While our cottage was in short walking distance, some of the delegates put up in a lodge near Malelane Gate 12km away were escorted to their accommodation by a couple of well armed rangers.

How vital precautionary measures like this could be, is narrated by Bruce Bryden in his book *A Game Ranger Remembers*. On one occasion a group of three lionesses was found strolling on the lawns of the guesthouse near the gate. They stayed on for a while not threatening anyone directly but nevertheless posing a serious danger to guests and staff. It was hoped they would move away before anything happened. Since they did not show any intention of doing so, there was no choice for the unfortunate rangers, and heavy-heartedly it was decided to destroy them.

The delegates, the next day, did not report having been waylaid by big cats, they had entered their chalets without being growled at.

Leaving a wonderful place

It was time to leave and head back north. It was only with reluctance that we left the camp in the bushveld.

Early afternoon, a spacious car drove up to give us and other delegates a lift to the airport 75km away. It took about one hour and a half to get to Nelspruit. Following a lengthy process of sorting out our tickets, the check-in clerk finally gave us our boarding passes through to London and sent us to what was called the lounge.

The waiting area of the very small airport was quite unusual. It was nothing but a fenced-in space in the open outside the check-in building. More remarkable, it was just next to the runway. We took a seat and waited for the boarding announcement. It felt like a pavement café where people observe people out on a promenade, watching and judging each other, sharing the latest gossip, while sipping an espresso or a glass of African red. Only this took place more or less on the tarmac where planes would land, take off and taxi past. However, none was arriving and none was departing while we sat there, a few small aircraft were parked in the distance. Nothing much was going on.

Our plane was sitting just opposite our chairs enjoying the attentions of the pilot. He had swung himself up onto the wings to make sure his aircraft was airworthy and ready for its next round of duty. When the external inspection was completed and the aviation fuel was replenished, the flight was ready for departure.

When I climbed the few steps, an attendant demanded I hand over my small bag since, he said, it was too big to go inside the cabin. I doubted it, but there was no way of getting into a discussion a few minutes before take-off. Having read about the frequent theft of passengers' small luggage, I removed a few important documents and surrendered it. Inside, it was plainly obvious that there was plenty of space for a very small cabin bag even in a smallish plane. After a smooth flight of about fifty minutes we touched down in Johannesburg, and I was reunited with my bag. Nothing had been taken out, and nothing put in.

With plenty of time before take-off back to Britain, we wandered around the departure area, had some last biltong and bought a bouquet of beautiful protea flowers. Relaxing for two hours in the business class lounge of South African Airways, we prepared for the long flight back to London.

At 10,000m, I had visions of poachers, jackals, oranges, monkeys. A car alarm went off, disturbing my slumbers. I realized, it was the gentle announcement that the plane was on its descent into Heathrow.

Back at our house, we found a note from our neighbour who had taken care of our plants. "Welcome back home. I hope you had a good time, Frank." I promised him I would include his words in a travelogue should I ever write one.

'You got ter kind o' shape 'em in yer eye'

Dassies, Zebras, and Wineries:
Along the Southern Coast

Our third trip along her southern regions evoked the gradual advance and colonisation by the Dutch and the British from the 17th century onwards, even more than the previous excursions to South Africa. It also gave us a chance to learn more about the country's fauna and see some animals we had not encountered before.

'How about another trip South?', I was asked one day, 'Two speaking engagements seem a good excuse for some exploring, wouldn't you think so?'

'A perfectly acceptable reason. More about the past then, and more creatures, that's fine with me.'

This time Peter's brother Greg was joining us for most of the journey.

Stepping off the overnight flight from London on British Airways, Peter and I arrived at Cape Town airport at about 8am on a sunny Saturday morning in September. Greg was due to arrive almost two hours after us. Considering the vagaries of air travel, we had arranged to meet up in the hotel.

A large and comfortable car awaited us at the airport car rental. I got behind the steering wheel, as usual, and we made our way to our lodgings.

At the Cape

We had booked an apartment in Green Point for two nights and moved right in. It was soon apparent that there was an issue with safety in the country. Security guards kept an eye on the door to the hotel building as well as on the entrance to its two-storey parking lot.

We had just returned from a trip to a nearby corner shop buying essentials for the fridge when we heard a knock on our door.

'Here I am. Glad to see you two.'

'Glad to see you, too. Cup of tea?'

Not on a direct flight to Cape Town, Greg's trip was much longer than ours. Instead of allowing him to rest, his brother talked him into some exercise in the sun.

Sun and fog

Knowing that bad weather was on its way, Peter rushed us up to Table Mountain at about noon in moderately hot 25°C. Everybody else seemed to know about the forecast. The access road to the aerial cableway was lined with parking cars, bumper to bumper.

A steep track up the mountain right under the path of the cable car began next to the station. It raised a few doubts; all the same, up we went. Other ill-informed climbers had also taken the vaguely discernible and stone-littered trail for the right path to the top. Like them, after a time we knew better. Because of the heat and the intense sunshine it was exhausting to get up the slope. Peter and Greg climbed up like mountain goats, unlike me. Reaching the foot of the mountain's cliffs we decided to split. It was agreed that I went back down to the station and up to the top in the gondola. They would attempt to get there via one of the official hiking routes, which they hoped to find in due time. As it turned out they did not.

I was on the top for about twenty minutes when they also appeared, by gondola. The track they had found looked slightly dangerous and was not the path they expected, so, ever so wise, they returned to the station. As we found out later, it would not have been the official ascent anyway. Only from the top did we discover where the path was running through the Platteklip Gorge. Following your exploring spirit does not always pay.

While waiting for Peter and Greg, I dashed into the small souvenir shop and left it with a lovely memento in the shape of a cheerful hand-painted mug. Together with my travelogue and many photos, in years to come, it will remind me of my stay at the Cape.

The yellow sun is shining brightly over the green mountain and black gondolas and the blue sea, where a yellow boat with white sails is bobbing in the waves, and a happy looking grey dolphin is enjoying himself with a smile on his face.

And I came out of the shop with a wide smile on mine.

In the footsteps of a lady and an official

So, at last the three of us were up on top of Table Mountain, overlooking the city, mountains, hills and bays. We stood in silent wonder at the immensity of the Atlantic Ocean in front of us and the endlessness of the horizon in the far distance.

I recalled Lady Anne Barnard, wife of the Colonial Secretary of the Cape Andrew Barnard, who had been standing at the same spot over 200 years ago: "Looking down on the town [...] with much conscious superiority."[30] We were as

---

[30]Letter 10.7.1797. The Letters of Lady Anne Barnard, p49. Whether this remark was meant as an endorsement of the superiority of the European culture as understood at the time, or simply as a description of her view across the bay, I cannot infer from the letter. Given her position in society, it might very well be the first.

high up as she had been, but the place we saw down there was not the same. She would not recognize it today. Since then, the town has grown from a victualling station and military outpost to a world renowned tourist destination and economic centre for trade and industries.

From 1087m above sea level we had a great view of Lion's Head with Lion's Rump, around which the city of Cape Town was winding its districts. The magnificent views over the town with its suburbs lined up along the shore were certainly the main reason to come up here besides the local flora and fauna.

Our vantage point offered a good view over the port and the adjoining bays. Container and cruise ships were berthed at the docks, tiny sailing boats took advantage of the winds. They all looked like toys from the viewing platform; speaking in the words of the Cape Governor's Private Secretary, they "dwindled away to the eye of the spectator into littleness and insignificance."[31] The ships which John Barrow saw from up here in the late 1790s were very different ships indeed, those were the British fleet guarding the newly acquired colony.

The wide plateau was covered with a beautiful meadow of low growing grass and bushes. Shining with shades of pale pink, swaths of fynbos dominated the vegetation. Growing mainly on poor soil, ericaceae and proteaceae belong to the species, that are rich in colour, form and habit.

Some need ropes, and some don't

The mountain had another attraction. A sizeable population of hyrax or dassies had made their home in the rocks and walls surrounding the viewing area. Called rock-rabbits by the early settlers, they were diurnal and gregarious, about the size of a rabbit with two long upper incisors. These fury mammals were living between the rocks, and in case of danger disappeared like lightning through gaps in the stone wall. Even the larger ones squeezed through with ease to Peter's amazement.

As the local residents, they had to bear with the daily intrusion of visitors into their territory. Making the most of the invasion, they sneaked up to the tourists demanding their dues. People were charmed by them and obliged gladly. The dassies also posed for photographs without being asked. Most of the time they were sitting on top of the wall soaking up the warm sunshine.

Though accustomed to the presence of humans whom they tolerated on their patch, they would perhaps not enjoy living really close to them as one of their relatives in Kenya did. Pati, the pet dassie of Joy Adamson, as described in

---

[31] An account of travels into the interior of southern Africa, I, p38.

her book about Elsa the lioness, travelled with her, slept on her bed, curled around her neck and was great friends with the three lion cubs.

There were quite a lot of visitors on the summit, taking advantage of the sunshine before the rains arrived. Like them, we rambled about the large area. But not for long because the notorious sheet of fog was approaching from the sea. With it the weather began to change. Mid afternoon it was getting noticeably cooler and clouds were moving in, accompanied by increasing winds.

We made our way to the cableway. But why was there a gathering of people standing at the perpendicular wall, staring down into the abyss? Had something happened?

Not yet, but something was about to.

A daring group of climbers of Abseil Africa, a local adventure organisation, was preparing for their own very particular method of getting back down, opting for a shortcut. They were making ready to descend the vertical wall. Not bothered by the changing conditions, they were standing right on the edge of the cliff, familiarizing their minds with the void at their feet. Their gear was piled in heaps around them: harnesses, boots, ropes, carabiners, bags, gloves and helmets.

When the climbers were getting serious, I did not wish to watch, hoping they would arrive at the bottom in one piece.

A cautious look from a safe distance at the forbidding precipice made me shudder. I preferred the more comfortable way of getting back down. Some of the visitors were following the preparations of the abseilers with curiosity, shaking their heads in disbelief. Such an adrenaline-driven descent was not for them either.

Watching the proceedings, a congregation of dassies did the same, with obvious incredulity wondering why people needed ropes and other implements to get down that rock-face.

Considering the weather it was time to leave the summit. Very soon, both the plateau and the view would be obscured by fog and we would start freezing. Others had come to the same conclusion.

Painlessly gliding down to the lower cableway station, we had a splendid view over most of the metropolitan area of Cape Town. From here, it was apparent that the city was not only dominated by the famous flat-topped mountain but also by the long-stretched ridge that reached right down into the residential suburbs. The road to the station was still bathed in sunshine, while the fog was creeping in on Signal Hill from the Atlantic. And that was exactly where we wanted to go next.

In order to do that, we had to find our rental car. Where was it? The row of vehicles had increased even more after we had arrived, now there were hundreds. And which one was it anyway?

'Wasn'it a black one?'

'No, rather grey it did look to me.'

'You mean, the colour of an elephant?'

'Something like that. Why not take this one, it looks nice?'

'You want to hijack the Abseil car? Better not.'

'Could be the one over there then. The key should know.'

'Et voilà, it does.'

Fowls on a political spot

The successful trip to the station shop and the masterly hunt for our vehicle emboldened us somewhat. While pondering the increasing fog with some doubts and wondering whether we really should plunge into it, we grew ever more determined to do just that.

We found the right turn to Signal Hill at the end of Lion's Rump, so called on account of its shape. Taking a deep breath, we drove into the white sheet.

By now the fog was so dense that we did not see beyond a few metres. Without a smile but with the utmost concentration following the course of the tarmac in front of the bonnet and a hard grip on the steering wheel, I inched the car forward along the road. Luckily, no vehicle came from the opposite direction, which would have been dangerous indeed, given the limited width of the road. Relieved and smiling, we made it to our goal without slipping down the mountain slope into the greyness.

Not a lion loitered at the parking lot but a group of handsome guineafowls, foraging for worms and insects on the lawn of the picnic area. Neither were they irritated by our presence, nor did they disperse in a panic. When we got out of the car for a few minutes, they did not interrupt their activities. They were rather cool.

There was no sound, except for the pecking of the birds. And there was no view whatsoever. We were engulfed by dense moist air. Heavy, humid and grey-white fog created an eerie atmosphere and induced a surreal feeling. Not knowing what is around, made me uneasy. And yet, we wanted to come here, fog or no fog, and fog was what we got, as could be expected. Whingeing was no option. Shrouded in a cloud of cold mist, it was hard to believe that a mere ten minutes and 300m away it was hot and sunny.

Signal Hill not only offered great views, in theory at least, its high-up location once served an important purpose for the town. In former times it was used as a signalling post. From the elevated position, signal flags transmitted information to arriving ships and also to the inhabitants, like weather warnings or instructions about the conditions in the harbour. Guns announced the arrival of a ship or alerted the population, when ships in the bay were in trouble.

The Hill was also a strategic point, in particular in times of conflict. When the Cape was fought over by the Dutch and the British, the geographical qualities of the place were more important than its beauty. Enemy forces "might get possession of the Lion's Rump [...] from whence, with a few howitzers, the town and citadel, and the strong batteries on the west side of Table Bay, would be completely commanded."[32]

The fowls certainly did not care about tactics, politics, strategies or even cannons but only what the soil had to offer them.

We made our way back to the junction just as slowly and carefully as before. Emerging from the obscuring veil and having defeated the fog, we saw that Table Mountain was still in full sunshine, but an extensive sheet of fog was closing in on it. The mountain, too, was soon to disappear.

We travelled back to Cape Town along the bay via Clifton, the city's exclusive suburb, and the equally wealthy district of Bantry Bay. Beautiful estates could be seen sited close to the shore surrounded by palm trees and facing the surf rolling in. The ocean stretched on our left while on our right was Signal Hill, still engulfed in fog.

Concluding our first day in South Africa, we had dinner in a restaurant near the hotel. Fortunately, the bed was not far away.

---

[32] John Barrow, An account of travels into the interior of southern Africa, II, p208.

A look back into the city's past

Cape Town is of course not only famous for its Table Mountain, but also for its place in history. On our journey along the southern coast of South Africa from West to East and back we found everywhere references to the Dutch and to the British period, their East India Companies and their international links in the Asia trade. It was mainly the Dutch that came our way.

We explored the town and its environs. I parked our car in Buitengracht; it was the only one in the parking area, as it was a Sunday morning. No one else was out and about. At this time of day and week the centre of town was all but deserted.

Our little walk through town was like gazing into a bygone era.

Cheerful colours with a shade of black

A few steps away, a small district evoked one particular aspect of the early years of European settlement. We strolled through the streets of the Bo-Kaap neighbourhood, a colourful part of town. Dating back to the late 18th century, the small single-storeyed flat-roofed houses were decorated in joyous colours ranging from bright green, yellow or pink to intense magenta. We noticed a number of mosques.

The area was known as the Malay Quarter. Here, descendants of Muslims from different regions of the East used to live, with Malay as their lingua franca. Most of their ancestors had not come here on their own free will. By force, they had been brought to the Cape by the Dutch East India Company from the 16th century onwards. They had been prisoners and political exiles as well as slaves.

Peeling away the bright paint reveals some dark facts, a closer look might shed some light on the veneer.

Scents, cannons and opposition

For centuries, Venetian, Ottoman, Arab, African, Indian, Chinese, Peranakan, Buginese and other merchants ran well established long-distance sea routes and caravan trails interlinking West and East. At the end of the 15th century, armed ships from Portugal, Spain and England started to appear in South East Asia keen on exploring new economic opportunities. In 1596 came the first Dutch.

The Malay Archipelago was abundant in spices such as cardamon, peppers, clove, nutmeg, mace, ginger, naming but a few. They were sought after for their alleged medicinal and aphrodisiac properties as well as for their aroma and flavour. Of the thousands of islands dotted around the waters between the Java Sea, South China Sea and the Indian Ocean, the Moluccas with the Bandas were the main suppliers but also Ceylon for cinnamon and Bengal for opium. Profits from trading in those commodities were enormous.

Following the lure of the valuable spice trade, the Dutch East India Company or the VOC (Vereenigde Oostindische Compagnie founded in 1602) endeavoured to gain the monopoly in the lucrative trade in Asian products and to remove European competition from the field, in particular the Portuguese who dominated in the Indian Ocean.

While Spain, Portugal and England maintained bases in the region and intermittently over decades were at war with each other and in particular with the Dutch, the VOC eventually became the main power in the spice business. They were supported by certain local rulers who pursued their own ends in doing so. The VOC also applied other methods: repression, intrigues, alliances, treaties as well as naval blockades or the destruction of plantations and villages. When political manoeuvering or firepower did not help, they resorted to incarceration, enslavement or banishment. It did not take long for the Dutch to also secure a firm position in the intra-Asian trade system. Within a short time, the commercial enterprise of the Dutch East India Company stretched from the Netherlands to Japan.

I have been at both ends of the VOC's trading empire. Not long after my visit to Cape Town, I stood in front of the magnificent building in Oude Hoogstraat which once housed the headquarters of their Amsterdam Chamber. A few months later, I was at the Chief Factor's residence on the tiny island of Deshima.

In 1619, the VOC occupied Jayakarta on Java, renamed it Batavia and made it their regional headquarters. In 1621, their conquest of the Banda Islands was complete. In the 1680s, they interposed in wars of succession in several sultanates, and in the 1740s, in another power struggle, they killed thousands of Muslim Chinese, whereupon a joint Javanese-Chinese army fought the Infidels from Europe. Those events reverberated as far as the Cape.

While local merchants and rulers resented the European interlopers, they did not hesitate to use the newcomers in their own power struggles, when they, on occasion, posed a threat to their interests and disrupted long-standing business ties. With the foreigners' ongoing meddling or intruding, a number of Muslim sovereigns and spiritual leaders did not appreciate the heavy-handed tactics of the VOC and opposed the interference of the Christian Dutch. Demonstrating their power, the Company's response was severe.

A number of leading religious and political officials, prominent noblemen and princes were captured, imprisoned and shipped to the southern tip of Africa.

Exporting spices, deporting troublemakers

Amid wafts of fragrant cinnamon and aromatic nutmeg, eminent scholars and distinguished figures found themselves on vessels of the Dutch fleet, banished to the African continent. Only a few were ever allowed to return. On arrival at the Cape, most were jailed and isolated. A few of those prisoners stand out.

Shaikh Muhammad Yusuf al-Maqassari, Islamic scholar and advisor to the sultan of Bantam on Java, following hostilities between the ruler and his son who was backed by the Dutch, was captured by the VOC in 1684. For ten years locked up in Batavia and Ceylon, in 1694, he disembarked at the Cape and was housed outside the town.

Among the noblemen expelled to the Cape, was, in 1722, a prince of Ternate in the Moluccas and, in 1746, a prince of Madura, an island off Java, for having joined an anti-VOC rebellion in 1745.

In 1744, an Imam of exalted status and lineage was seized by the Company's officers on Java. A descendant from the Prophet, Sayyed Alawie al-Hashimi al-Arabie was a person of great authority. Allegedly, he had encouraged killing the foreigners and demanded the conversion of the Dutch to Islam. In 1747, he was sent to Robben Island. Released eleven years later, Alawie found himself appointed a constable in Cape Town.

In 1780, another leading figure arrived from the Spice Islands as a state prisoner. Said to have conspired with the English against the Dutch during the Fourth Dutch-English War, Imam Abdullah ibn Qadi Abdus Salaam was imprisoned on Robben Island for thirteen years. On his release in 1793, he moved to Bo-Kaap where several Free Muslim slaves owned land. On one of those plots, he founded a Muslim school and the first mosque and, now also called

Tuan Guru, taught the Quran. His initiatives were the beginnings of what later became the so-called Malay Quarter.

Robben Island in Table Bay, initially serving as a source
for penguin and seal meat for the first Dutch colonists in
the 16th century, was used as a jail for political convicts
in the 17th and 18th century. Inmates not only came from
the Company's stations in the East but also from the set-
tler community at the Cape and from local tribes. The
British also used it as a penal colony. In the 20th century,
the island grew to world notoriety when Nelson Mandela
was incarcerated there for eighteen years, as graphically
described in his autobiography *Long Walk to Freedom*.

Peppers and slaves on board

Sailing West, the large ships of the VOC were loaded with
opium, horns, tin, salt, coffee, porcelain as well as chests
of spices and bales of chintz and silks for the European
market. They also transported a very different kind of cargo
destined for the Cape: slaves.

Since times immemorial, slaving had been accepted practice in Nordic, Arabian, Indian, Asian and African countries. The traditional slaving networks were multi-directio-
nal systems, reaching from the West and North of Africa
and Europe to the East and South-East of Asia. Operating within international networks, the merchants ran a
wide-spread interconnecting maritime and overland business scheme. Whether handling goods or humans along
their age-old trading structures, the destination for onward
transport were exchange markets or important seaports.

Dealing in slaves relied on proven procedures. Operations to purchase human supply relied on sultans, khans,
kings, tribal chiefs, traders and their agents, who maintained a finely tuned web of intermediaries. Slaves were

obtained through a variety of deals, exchanged for goods, sold on in money transactions, but also through kidnapping, raiding and during inter-tribal wars. The captured men, women and children were also taken as payment of war indemnity or used as a commodity in a barter system as bonded labour to pay for loans in an elaborate net of debt and obligation. At times, captives served as objects for sacrifices in funeral ceremonies. In most cases, they were auctioned on large slave markets to the highest bidder.[33]

The Dutch, like other European countries, were involved in the slave trade from the late 1500s at least. One location for the VOC to source their slaves was Batavia and its environs. Half its population were slaves of diverse origin, religion, ethnicity and customs. Macassar was also a notorious slave-market, and in the Malacca region slaves could easily be obtained. When defeating a town or a sultanate, the Dutch often enslaved the population wholesale. Slaves were shipped to the Cape as needed, sold there to settlers and VOC employees, or they came as household slaves of officials. Some remained slaves and some did not.

Several examples may illustrate how such slaves managed to improve their lot dramatically. Social mobility within the Cape's world was possible and there were ways for slaves to better their life: they were set free as a reward for their loyalty and hard work, or they could replace themselves with another slave and leave, or they were able to buy their own freedom with money they had earned. A few remarkable female slaves should be mentioned.

---

[33]The notes of an African slave trader in the 18th century in what is today's Nigeria are most informative; see Stephen Behrendt *The diary of Antera Duke*. The operations of a slave trader and his using and abusing a young boy pawned to pay his father's debt is the subject, among others, of the novel *Paradise* by Abdulrazak Gurnah. The author was awarded the Nobel Prize in literature in October 2021.

In 1657 a Dutch fleet brought a slave family who had been captured in the Ganges area. Owned by a Batavian landdrost they were sold to van Riebeeck, who, when he left the Cape in 1662, sold all of them to a deputy commander, who, in 1666, freed Angela van Bengal and her children. She was baptized and married a Free Burgher. She became a successful entrepreneur, owned livestock, land, farms, and slaves and she established the first fishing business at the Cape.

Her daughter Anna de Koningh, whose father was a Dutch captain, in 1678 married Olof Bergh, a VOC employee. At his death in 1724, among other properties she became the owner of Groot Constantia and more than two dozen slaves until her own death in 1733.

Coridon van Ceylon, freed by his owner, had purchased land in what is now the Bo-Kaap area. His wife, also a freed slave, inherited the property and sold it to their daughter Saartje van de Kaap, who donated a warehouse on the plot to be used by Tuan Guru as the first mosque at the Cape. She married his successor, Imam Achmat from West Bengal, a fact that enhanced her standing considerably.

When not importing slaves to the new station from the Malay Archipelago or from the Straits of Malacca and their posts in Bengal, Gujarat or Ceylon, the Dutch East India Company procured them from the African continent. They acquired them wherever they could, by whichever ways, whether along the west coast or in the ports of Madagascar, from their station on Mauritius or via Zanzibar, the principal collection and transshipment point for slaves on the east coast.[34]

---

[34] In his book *The last slave market*, Alastair Hazell recounts the history of the East African slave trade, outlining the importance of Zanzibar's far-reaching trading network into central Africa, all of Arabia and the Gulf countries and across the Indian Ocean.

The first commander of the Cape settlement, Johan An-
thoniszoon van Riebeeck, before taking up his post in April
1652, held positions in the VOC organisation at Batavia
and Deshima. Recording on a daily basis the developments
in the new settlement, his journals frequently refer to slaves
from Africa rather than to those from the East.

Van Riebeeck owned some slaves, like other Dutch at
the station. In March 1655 he complained that one of his
own slaves had disappeared: "It is now several days since
we first missed a certain Madagaskar slave, and we do not
know where he has gone." A few months later he states "so
long as we have no slaves". With a shortage of labourers
and helpers, missing slaves had to be replaced.

In 1658, two vessels arrived carrying African slaves that
had been snatched from rival slave ships. 250 were landed
at the Cape in March: "Male and female slaves brought
here from Angola by the Amersfoort, which had taken them
from off [sic] a prize Portuguese slaver." In May, the next
batch of 228 slaves arrived. At the end of September only
83 slaves were left. The journal reveals that the settlers
lost them through sickness, death and desertion with the
latter as the main cause: "Every day it becomes more ev-
ident that the Guinea and Angola slaves are inclined to
desert", the governor lamented in August. Previously 28
had absconded. With the number of slaves oscillating, re-
supplying or extending their stock proved to be an ongoing
necessity.[35]

The British, ruling over the Cape after the Dutch, kept
slaves on a larger scale. In May 1800, in a letter to Henry
Dundas, Secretary for War and the Colonies, Lady Barnard
referred to the arrival of a substantial number of slaves from

---

[35]Van Riebeeck's Journal I, 12.3.1655 (p300) und 8.8.1655 (p335).
Van Riebeeck's Journal II, 17.4.1658 (p258) und 28.8.1658 (p329).

the east African coast: "Liberty to import 1600 slaves, but to land here a supposed prize cargo [...] the slaves realy [sic] having been purchased at Mozambique."[36] Only a few years later, in 1807, Britain prohibited the slave trade. Well into the 20th century, local San were also used as Laurens van der Post, haunted by his ancestors' part in reducing the bushmen, relates in his book *The Lost World of the Kalahari.*

Victualling station on the Asia run

We strolled along Long Street, one of the oldest streets in town with its shops, travel agencies, restaurants and clubs, Victorian buildings and beautiful balconies. No one else could be seen, and, regrettably, the bookshops were closed. When the British novelist Anthony Trollope visited in the late 1870s, he remarked that "Capetown is not specially dirty – but it is somewhat ragged. The buildings are not grand, but there is no special deficiency in that respect. [...] But the town is not pleasing to a stranger."[37] Walking along the streets and finding the town rather nice, we arrived at the opposite conclusion.

A midway stop to save lives

We came to the Company's garden which had played a major role in the history of the Cape. Cape Town was founded by the Dutch East India Company as a replenishing post on their Asian trading route. A reliable supply station for clean water and fresh food was vital on long sea voyages

---

[36] 14.5.1800. The Letters of Lady Anne Barnard, p240. Most British slaves came from Mozambique at the time.

[37] South Africa, vol I, p50.

that took many months if not years. Soon after the establishment of the Company, the importance of the right food for morale and survival of the crews as well as for the safety of the precious ships and their valuable cargo was put to the directors, the Heren XVII.

Admiral Cornelis Matelieff de Jonge, lifetime director in the Rotterdam Chamber of the Company, was fleet commander of the VOC's second voyage to South-East Asia. After a run of three and a half years he returned in the autumn of 1608 with a reduced number of vessels and a decimated contingent of mariners. In a paper to the Board of Directors he emphasized the dangerous lack of appropriate nourishment for the sailors, and he suggested to establish bases at strategic locations along the Asia route.

Only a healthy crew, mentally and physically, was able to operate and protect their ship in a potentially hostile environment. Therefore, the quality of food was of paramount importance. The supplies that had been loaded prior to departure in Europe gradually lost their nutritional value and tended to go bad, often even before the East was in sight. After a few weeks at sea, salted meat, ship's biscuits, bread or cheese were spoilt, and water was smelling foul. Fresh produce soon rotted away. The closer the ship came to its final destination in the eastern seas, the more worrying the situation became. Food readily turned mouldy in the tropical climate, but what had not yet deteriorated entirely was maintained for emergencies.

Access to fresh provisions was more of a problem on the return voyage than on the outward sailing, even though new stock was taken on board before leaving the East. Those supplies did not last long enough to reach the ship's final destination back in Europe. The crew had to rely on the months-old food, packed into the hold before departure in the West. The consequences were serious. The nearer the fleets got to their home port, the more alarming their dietary problems became: "What kills people is the old food which we use when we near this country [...] in the vicinity of our cold country, the bodies receive no nutrition from the old food." He had seen how devastating and deadly rotten food was: "Because it is a pity to see the crew die before one's eyes. I would not use meat from the fatherland on the return voyage." In his experience, adequate nutriment was a highly pressing issue which had to be addressed urgently. The admiral recommended to build store houses at supply points, "where we can gradually gather all provisions (food, ammunition for warfare and other necessities), so that all ships that wish to leave for the fatherland can take aboard all kinds of fresh victuals there." [38]

The crew not only had to be in a reasonable state of health in order to cope with the long months at sea. The sailors also had to be able to defend the invaluable cargo in their vessel's hold in case of attacks from pirates or rival East India Companies' ships as well as from naval fleets of unfriendly local or European powers.

Considering the distances involved and the fact that currents and winds often forced fleets to wait many days or weeks for more favourable sailing conditions around the bay of the future Cape Town, the Cape offered everything as to strategic location, suitable harbour and vital supplies, both outbound and inbound. Many years later, it fell to van Riebeeck to turn Matelieff's proposition and the Company directors' instructions into reality at the point where the sea route between Europe and Asia rounded the African continent.

---

[38] Journals, memorials and letters of Cornelis Matelieff de Jonge, p304. Deficiency diseases and their dietary treatment have been recognized in China at least from the 14th century.

Adhering to the admiral's advice, in the first year of his ten year tenure at the Cape, the governor established a fruit and vegetable plot. The Company's garden was the place in town I was interested to see the most.

Curing sick mariners

When the Dutch pushed into equatorial zones, their merchant and military fleets faced unknown challenges. Long-distance voyages that might take years to complete were always hazardous and never far from calamities of any sort. The admiral's own first-hand experience taught the VOC that expeditions into the tropics necessitated a new approach as to the health of the men on board and the logistics of the operations. The humid climate with steaming rain and oppressive heat, conspiring with diseases like typhoid, dysentery, cholera and malaria put the crews under severe strain. Apart from further threats like violent storms and enemy ships, it was the crew's deficient diet which might put the whole voyage in grave danger.

Scurvy regularly crippled the crews on long sea voyages. Symptoms of the disease are weakness, joint and leg pain, bleeding gums, bruising skin or even organ failure. In 1617, a publication by John Woodal, surgeon to the English East India Company, advocated a diet of vegetables and citrus fruit to prevent the disease. 1654 van Riebeeck reported in his journal how afflicted mariners were cared for at the station: "This afternoon we had all the sick and scorbutics, about 60 in number, brought ashore [...] in order to treat them so well with cabbages and other potherbs for their refreshment every day, that they may soon with God's help be on their feet again."[39] But only in the mid 1700s, in trials by James Lind, surgeon in the Royal Navy, scurvy

---

[39]10.7.1654. Van Riebeeck's Journal I, p249.

was proven conclusively to be a nutritional disease caused by a deficiency of Vitamin C, an essential nutrient found mainly in fruits and vegetables.

Protein was also a necessary component in the diet to maintain general health. With game plentiful at the Cape, there was no lack of meat for the passing ships and the new settlement. From the beginning they also had livestock like pigs, cattle and poultry. Fish, mussels and other seafood as well as birds were also readily available for the new arrivals.

The sailors depended as much on supplementing their provisions from the governor's garden as the settlers on restocking their larders with new deliveries from the ships. Despite the productive garden and their agricultural products, the colonists at times were running low on supplies: "Contrary to our expectations, the return fleet has passed us by, and we find ourselves at present very scantily provided and almost entirely destitute of daily victuals."[40]

What remained of the once vital and well-kept Company's garden was not a kitchen garden anymore. Disappointingly, it offered a neglected sight. The garden we walked through looked desolate, it certainly did not reflect the purposeful enthusiasm with which the original plot had been maintained. It had a sorry look about it with squares of tired lawn, badly kept tarmac paths, and wilfully damaged branches. The tall trees seemed to be old and might have been planted a long time ago: "The commander [...] ordered young trees of a certain kind [...] to be brought daily from the forest to be planted around the Company's gardens [...] to provide shelter from the strong squalls to which we are here subject."[41] I liked to think that these trees were dating back to van Riebeeck's time.

---

[40]27.4.1654. Van Riebeeck's Journal I, p232.
[41]9.7.1657. Van Riebeeck's Journal II, p128.

On a board at the entrance to the gardens a list of don'ts had been put up to dissuade people from doing what we witnessed them doing. Visitors were supposed to refrain from cutting down trees and digging up flowers. While we were there a group of about six local youths were busy breaking the large leaves of some flowers, few there were anyway. I was upset about this pointless and stupid action. Van Riebeeck would be very angry, I thought.

Army and arts in a fortress

Continuing our explorations we walked to the Castle of Good Hope. The first things the arrivals from Holland had to do, besides building cabins, huts, storerooms and stables, was constructing a fort for defence. It was originally located at the seashore in front of the settlement and in good view of the ships that approached the midway station. The fort was meant to guard the newly established VOC outpost, deter attacks from the water and give easy access to sick or starving crews.

Made in 1652, the initial structure of clay, mud and timber, collapsed a few years later, as the builders had not reckoned with an assault by the weather. It was replaced ten years later with more suitable material. The new fort was built of stone to more effectively withstand rain, wind and storms and to better protect the growing town. The building was designed as a fortress, and it was never attacked. It is the best preserved piece of architecture of the 17th century, it is said to be the oldest colonial building existing in the country today.

The Castle of Good Hope is a fortification in the shape of a pentagon. Based on construction principles of military architecture and following mathematical and geometrical rules, it is a star-shaped construction with five bastions, high walls, a glacis and a wide ditch all round. Today, not much is left of the moat, most of the castle is squeezed in by busy roads. It is easy to see what impressive a structure it was then and still is after more than 360 years.[42]

Access was over the moat to the gated entry with its bell tower and on to a courtyard. The fort was divided into sections, housing offices, living quarters and prison cells. There were even trees and lawns doubling up as a parade ground.

Today the fortress is used by the South African Army; parts of it had been turned into a museum. One wing related to the history of the Cape, while another showcased an art collection.

In the colonial section, military artefacts, weapons and uniforms from the Dutch and British periods of the Cape were on display. Maps indicated the extent of the settlers' expansion and pinpointed the numerous places of skirmishes between the tribes and the colonists.

A most interesting display showed a network of signalling posts to convey information from one station to the next by using fire, smoke, flags or lamps. As on Signal Hill, this method was adopted to announce approaching ships, foe or friend. The system was also used to relay orders and communicate messages between the posts.

Another part of the museum housed a once private collection of paintings, furniture and artefacts from various periods. Comparing the paintings featuring Table Mountain showed an illuminating variety of ways representing it.

---

[42]The pentagonal or the polygonal concept was not only applied to the construction of fortifications but also in the design of European towns of the 16th and 17th century. Examples are Rocroi in France (1555), Palmanova in Italy (1593), Coevorden in The Netherlands (1597), Charleroi in Belgium (1666), Mannheim (1606) and Saarlouis (1680) in Germany.

In the beginning of the settlement, European artists worked from descriptions and without ever having seen their object with their own eyes. Over time, the artists came to know more of its actual form, through written or personal reports, some even travelling there, and more and more details were being reproduced on canvas. First it was represented just as a flat-topped piece of rock, later accurate note was taken of its slopes, escarpments and shape.

Ambling through the city and seeing those places referred me straight back onto the pages of van Riebeeck's detailed journal, and his remarks jumped right out of his diary. What I saw connected me to his almost daily jottings which gave revealing glimpses into his thoughts, but also acknowledged the burden of his task and the responsibility his position had put on him.

Happy with our findings so far, we made our way back to our still lonely car.

Gardens, grapes and penguins

A drive of some twenty minutes brought us to Kirstenbosch National Botanical Gardens. The area was not only interesting from a botanical point of view but also from a historical perspective.

From forest to country seat to botanical garden

In October 1657, the Dutch had discovered a piece of forest quite a distance away from the settlement. Roads were built to exploit the abundance of timber. Vast stretches of trees were felled to be used as urgently needed building material and firewood.

One of the settlers, Leendert Cornelis, established a farm there, which until the end of the 18th century was called Leendertsbos. When it changed hands, it was enlarged and the name was changed to Kirstenbos. Subsequently, the estate had various owners the latest of whom was Cecil Rhodes, entrepreneur and the Cape's Prime Minister from 1890 to 1896. In 1913 the large area was turned into a botanical garden that has gained worldwide recognition and attracts thousands of visitors.

The road leading to the entrance of the gardens was lined with trees which the prime minister had planted. They have grown into tall trees in more than one hundred years. Majestic Camphor trees with their glossy leaves and Moreton Bay figs, a spreading strangler fig, as well as Spanish chestnuts lined the elegant avenue.

'What a shame, he cannot see the results.'

'It would probably please him to see how they have matured.'

'Think of the grand parks of Europe or the gardens in the temple complexes of Japan. Those who designed them and those who planted them up never saw their work in full bloom, since the plants took decades even centuries to reach their peak.'

His wonderful trees provided a lot of shade during hot summer hours. On a greyish day like this without much sunshine and some likely rain, their leaves, their branches and their outspreading crowns offered protection.

Compared to the trees in the Company garden, the prime minister's trees were not truly old at all. Yet, I was wondering what Mr. Rhodes' trees had witnessed over the course of a hundred odd years, and what stories they could tell. Unfortunately, I was not conversant in tree whisper.

Intruders' versus locals' interest

The main purpose of our visit was to follow up on a further entry in van Riebeeck's notes. We made our way to the higher slopes of the huge garden. Soon I found what I was looking for.

It was another testimony to the governor's initiatives to make the Company's midway post at the Cape viable: a deep hedge of immense tangled thickness. In February 1660, he noted in his journal his intention to mark and protect the boundaries of the settlement by planting an impenetrable hedge around it, consisting of "bitter almond trees and all sorts of fast-growing brambles and thornbushes." By this means their livestock would be kept in and unwanted visitors kept out, human or animal. "This belt will then be so densely overgrown that it will be impossible for cattle or sheep to be driven through and it will take the form of a protective fence, like those with which some lords and squires mark off the boundaries of their territories in certain parts of Germany and in the district of Cologne."[43] A few hundred years later, I stood at the very obstruction the governor had planned. A few chunks of it have survived to this day and are still going strong.

The governor's idea was soon put into practice, and over time, the trees, shrubs and plants chosen developed into just the formidable barrier he had envisaged. The strong branches of the almond trees, the spearlike spikes of the thornbushes together with the interplanted shrubs were meant to put off anybody from attempting to penetrate this kind of fencing. Most likely, one of the ingredients the labourers used for the project were hawthorn saplings, the ideal plant to construct fast growing hedgerows, as well as other suitable hedging plants. Some species may have

---

[43]25.2.1660. Van Riebeeck's Journal III, p185-186.

been added in the shape of seeds in the droppings of birds that found refuge within the growing structure, together with insects, reptiles and small mammals. Interwoven over the centuries and interconnected through underground fungal networks and root systems, they have matured into a living wall.

Looking at this prickly masterpiece, I was wondering how effective those plants could have been while they were in their phase of settling in, requiring years to get established. When put into the soil they were probably just useful as the marking of the boundary, considering how long it took to form such a barricade, in particular when taking into account the reasons the hedge was planted in the first place.

The sections of the governor's impressive hedge planted 360 years ago, that are still in existence, are in a manner of speaking a living witness to the clashes between the foreign settlers and the native inhabitants.

The background for the scheme were disputes with the local tribes that had simmered for a few years and boiled over in open conflict in 1659. The area which was taken over and constantly extended by the Dutch was in fact the grazing land of the Khoi. At first, they had been happy to barter with the new arrivals for meat or livestock. When they realized, however, that the Dutch were rigorously invading their space rather than merely trading, the tribes attacked to regain their traditional territory. They were defeated, and a peace treaty was agreed. The Khoi were restricted in their movements, the Company retained the lands they had taken from them.

The VOC went on to push their settlement farther into the ancestral lands of the Khoi in more confrontations with them and other tribes.

A dazzling show on a grey day

Not many visitors were in the sprawling grounds of Kirstenbosch on this greyish day, in most places we had the garden to ourselves. It was not raining yet, but the sky did not inspire confidence. We did not have umbrellas anyway, so had to ignore the probability of raindrops falling from the skies.

Table Mountain could be seen from all points of the park, offering a spectacular background for the garden design and the rich collection of plants.

We ambled along the pathways and flower beds and across the lawn areas. Strolling along, we appreciated the tireless work of the gardeners, who kept the beds in immaculate order and the grass manicured to perfection and the bushes clipped to look their best. Our own garden did not look as good as this one; the distance to Britain was just too far to hire those skillful garden experts.

The varied vegetation of the park testified to the botanical diversity supported by the South African climate. The palette of plants included all native specimen, as it was the aim of the organisation that runs Kirstenbosch to cultivate all members of the indigenous flora. The flowerbeds were packed with plants of every description, intense splashes of colour added some drama among the rich greenery. Sweeping drifts of fynbos, the heathland vegetation of the Cape, formed a resplendent carpet of hues lighting up the dullish weather. There were also slow-growing succulents like euphorbia and pachypodium, adapted to survive in arid environments. In one section of the park the intense scent of some plants made us halt and inhale their fragrance. There were beds with medicinal plants. There were also some trees like beech and stinkwood.

We arrived at a small pool. Most of the plants growing in its marginals were plain green but one stood out.

A cluster of stands caught my eye because of its attractive colour mix. The arrangement of shapes and lines as well as the combination of soft hues looked like a beautiful painting. I liked the appealing symphony of that harmony of shades. Tall green stems had leaves of an orange-brown colour, and some had a kind of tuft at their tip.

I assumed it to be paper reed or papyrus sedge, a native of the African continent. A fast growing perennial, it sat in a large clump in shallow water at the edge of the well-stocked pond.

We left this famous place of horticulture and turned our attention to the topic of viticulture.

Hospitality in a wine glass

Constantia Valley not far away was a region with many small and large wineries. The mild climate with plenty of rain and cool breezes offered great potential, and, from early on, the vineyards became renowned for their excellent grapes and wines. The full bodied dessert wines of Groot Constantia were famous and appreciated by kings and poets from early on. Because of its significance and history we wanted to visit this particular wine estate, since 1984 a National Monument.

The celebrated vineyards were not open but the grand mansion was. Destroyed by fire in 1925, it had been rebuilt in the following years. Traditional furniture, paintings, and household goods were arranged for visitors to see. Life in the house seems to have been very comfortable. In one of the adjacent buildings a collection of coaches and displays of drinking glasses and bottles were arranged. The exhibition bore witness to the lavish sociability and entrepreneurial spirit of the owners as well as to the important position of the estate in the business and social circles of the colony. In a separate room a brief history of Groot Constantia was given, illustrated by a small sketch of the farm by Lady Anne Barnard showing how the buildings looked like in May 1798.

The large fields and gardens had required a large work-force, and, as on other landholdings at the Cape, that were slaves. Slaves were essential in the running of the colony, and that applied to Groot Constantia as well. They not only worked as farm labourers but also in various domestic positions. Some were able to alter their status before the general emancipation in 1834.

A look at some of the owners of Groot Constantia reveals interesting facts.

The estate had been established in 1685 by Simon van der Stel, before he became governor of the Cape for seven years until 1699. He was the son of Adriaan van der Stel, second governor of the Dutch settlement on Mauritius from 1640 to 1645 and his Batavian wife, thought to be a former slave or the daughter of a slave and a Dutch sea captain.

In 1716, Groot Constantia was acquired by a Swedish employee of the VOC, Olof Bergh, who, following a brush with the law, was imprisoned on Robben Island for two years together with his family, and in 1690 sent to the VOC's station on Ceylon with his wife and children. Returning to the Cape in 1695, he bought several farms. On his death in 1724, the estates were transferred to his widow Anna de Koningh, a former slave.

Between 1778 and 1885 the estate was owned by five generations of the Cloete family. They had owned other farms before taking over the run-down buildings and vineyards, which they restored and replanted. A visitor to Groot Constantia during that period was impressed by the great care being bestowed on the wines and by the quality of the cellars, "Mr. Pluter's wine vaults are very extensive and neatly laid out, and every thing is in much better order than at any other wine farm I have seen."[44] He was more interested in what was in his glass than what his host's correct name was, which would have been Hendrik Cloete. Captain Percival was among the British troops who, during the Napoleonic Wars, took the Cape from the Dutch in 1796 only to enjoy their wine a little later. In 1885, the estate was sold to the Cape Government; it has been run by various organisations and trusts ever since.

The winery by now has developed into a commercial enterprise with huge metal silos, restaurants, museums and parking lots for tour busses. It was a busy and efficiently run place that attracted plenty of visitors.

We did not take part in any wine tasting, and I did not acquire another mug, but we should have bought a bottle of their famous wine. That omission required a future visit to the wine merchants of London.

Penguins don't care for history

We drove on to Muitzenberg, a seaside town in False Bay where in 1795 skirmishes had taken place, when the British

---

[44]Robert Percival, An Account of the Cape of Good Hope, p186.

invaded the Dutch Cape for the first time. The Cape was returned to the Dutch in 1802, only to be attacked for a second time in 1806 and to remain British until 1910.

From the coastal road we watched a couple of whales cruising in the bay. The animals have been coming to these waters for thousands of years. However, in modern times, the place has become far more in demand for surfing than for its history or whale watching.

The next town along the bay, Simon's Town, was named after Governor Simon van der Stel. Initially a shipyard of the Dutch East India Company since 1743, it became home to the British Royal Navy after the second occupation in 1806, and is today the base of the South African Navy.

Peter was impatient to get to the penguin colony in Boulders. The black and white Jackass penguins had started to settle here only a few decades ago. Today, they are an endangered species because their main source of food is decreasing due to overfishing.

When the Dutch arrived at the Cape, penguins were found on Robben Island. While today, they live in a safe sanctuary on the island, in former times their existence was a rather precarious one:

"The boat brought back on our instructions some penguin and seal meat to see whether the pigs could be fed with it [...] we shall be compelled to fetch penguins for the men to eat."[45] The entry in the governor's journal indicates the unpredictability and unreliability of their daily life at Table Bay.

Already in the car park the penguin's chatter could be heard. So we only had to follow their calls and walk along the narrow footpath behind the penguin community. Willis

---

[45] 4.4.1654. Van Riebeeck's Journal I, p225.

Walk separated the birds from the residential area or rather prevented them from invading the land above the shore even more.

On our left the human inhabitants were tucked away in their quiet houses behind hedges and walls, on our right the small feathered residents were growling and hissing noisily. From behind the wire fence they chatted to the passing visitors and to each other. Beneath the low shrubs the ground had been trampled solid by their feet; accumulated white guano deposits covered the soil. The burrows were closely packed since this was a very large colony with over 3,000 pairs.

From a boardwalk running down almost to the water's edge and ending in a viewing platform we got to within a few metres of the birds. From here we observed what was going on. Penguins were diving into the sea, shuffling out of the shallow water, waddling in the sand, talking to each other, walking to their nesting areas, and looking up inquisitively at those people who had come from all over the world to look down at them just as curiously.

Two of them were fed up with the noisy visitors, their camera clicks and their endless posing for selfies. Sulking, they turned their backs on us. They did not wish to have anything to do anymore with an overwhelming human crowd, who did not appreciate the pressure they endured on a daily basis. Heated disputes with the ever present neighbours over space, conflicts over nesting sites, arguments about where to sit down in the overcrowded penguin village.

Enough was enough for the duo. Staring into the sand was much nicer than being stared at.

Rubbish raiders' fun

Our visit was cut short when a heavy downpour started without much warning. We reached the car just before getting soaked to the skin. Even though it had become cold, grey, darkish, windy and wet, we stuck to our route planned for the day.

Undeterred, we continued our trip around the Cape Peninsula. Greg would have preferred to return to our dry hotel, but was overruled by the navigator and the driver. We got to the gate of the Cape of Good Hope Nature Reserve well before closing time. Because of the bad weather it was already locked. The rain had subsided a little in the meantime, but there was nothing we could do. Disappointed, we drove on, taking the coastal road back to Cape Town on the M65/M6 passing Kommetjie and Hout Bay.

Soon our setback was offset by some wild and destructive entertainment. Our attention was attracted by hectic activities near the road somewhere along the way. We parked on the kerbside and watched.

A group of boisterous baboons was in high spirits it seemed. They were busy raiding the rubbish bins of what appeared to be a small factory in one of the settlements. Behind the perimeter of the estate, they passed their time by wreaking havoc. Diving into the containers, they pulled out the contents and hurled the trash around the yard. Other bins were keeled over, and the waste was thrown everywhere. Perched on the branches of a tall tree within the premises, some of them watched the proceedings with interest. Those who were not engaged in the fun, climbed over the fence of the plant and crossed the road, disappearing into the vegetation. Satisfied with the chaos they had created, the horde retreated to the back buildings where we did not see them any longer.

Their handiwork was admirable, and we were wondering who would be tasked with cleaning up the mess and putting everything back in order. The factory headman was certainly not pleased about the baboon's wicked sense of humour.

We dined in a seafood restaurant in Camps Bay not very far from our accommodation. Following the recommendation of the sommelier at Berry Bros. & Rudd's of London, Britain's oldest wine and spirit merchants, we ordered a bottle of Hamilton Russell white wine to go with our seafood platters. Our plan for the next day included a visit to that very winery. The waiter, taking us for connoisseurs, or so we hoped, and appreciating our informed choice of wine, went on to praise the wines of Meerlust Wineries of Stellenbosch. In his view, their wines were the best there were. Taking note of the expert's advice we hoped to visit this estate as well. Unfortunately, a trip to their wine cellars did not work out, instead, we had to make do with a few bottles of their Chardonnay acquired in a wine shop later during the journey. After the sumptuous meal and the fine wine, regrettably just a sip for the chauffeur, we were back in the hotel in good time to fall into bed.

Thirteen hours later we left Cape Town.

Heading east

Passing through a few suburbs, we drove east on the M3/N2. As we had experienced before, locals were walking on the hard shoulder of the roads, even crossing the motorway. But on this highway it was worse. Lorries and vehicles moved to the hard shoulder to let faster cars pass. This did not deter people from using the same part of the road, seemingly unconcerned.

Whales, wines and well-mannered geese

In Botrivier we took the exit for Hermanus. A huge estate was being built at the outskirts of the town. Before constructing any houses, a three metres high stone wall had been erected right around the entire plot. An entrance gate with two small towers housing the security guards had also been built already. No houses were there yet but piles of building material which needed protection from theft. A high wall was more important than putting up the residences. Security came first in South Africa.

A number of small signposts depicting tail fins were leading to the coastal path from where to watch out for whales. We ended up on a small outlook near the coastal boulders of the cliff walk, overlooking the bay. And right down there in front of the car were the whales.

Greg and Peter went for a rainy walk along the wet track, but I stayed in the dry car. Through my binoculars I could see a large parking space and viewing area far from where we were. Considering the crowds, this appeared to be the official area where visitors were supposed to gather for watching tail fins. I was glad we had our private and quiet viewing point.

At the wrong place but not at the wrong spot.

Exchanging courtesies with white feathers

Not far from Hermanus we turned off to the R320 into the beautiful Hemel-en-Aarde Valley on the road to Caledon. The red dirt road was running through a delightful region of undulating hills, lush meadows and green hedges. Owing to the quality of the soil, a number of wine estates has sprung up. What was once forest and agricultural land, has been planted up with vines.

It was the grapevines that drove us here, namely those that produced delicious fermented grape juice on the terroir of the award-winning Hamilton Russell Vineyards. Considered among the finest wines in the world, all their wines were grown, harvested, pressed, matured, bottled and labelled on the estate. We pulled up at the small cottage serving as their tasting venue. Greg and Peter went in ahead of me.

Approaching the path to the cottage, I met a group of polite yet cautious geese. They were coming from the right intending to cross the paved path between me and the house. I stopped to wait for them walk across. They also stopped, discussed the situation among themselves, and decided it was not appropriate to carry on. Observing the etiquette of hospitality, they meant me, the guest to the estate, to cross first and, thank you, so I did smiling at them. The white party were either well brought up geese or timid creatures; appreciating their manners, I am sure they were more of the first with some prudence thrown in. While the courteous birds waddled across the path after I had passed, I proceeded further down a few steps to the cottage.

There I found my companions and a sommelier, who introduced the three of us to the estate and its wines. We found ourselves in a welcoming reception room with an array of bottles and glasses arranged on a big table. I once attended a wine tasting by the world renowned critic, co-author of *The World Atlas of Wine* and Master of Wine Jancis Robinson. Also owning two of her books, however, did not make me knowledgeable enough about all facets of wine. I guess he soon realized that we were not exactly experts in the matter but still able to appreciate fine wines. Following a tasting exercise of swirling, sniffing and sipping Peter bought a Pinot Noir and a Chardonnay. Homemade honey, made from local fynbos, was also acquired. Sweetened with the fine flavour, our daily dose of tea was now to taste even richer. Thanking us for the trouble we as individual travellers had taken to make our way to the winery, the sommelier proved to be just as gracious as the considerate geese.

Besides offering excellent soil, terrain and climate conditions for producing fine wines, the region was perfectly suited for breeding horses. Elegant creatures were almost floating around large paddocks. They looked like thoroughbreds or race horses. Judging from their numbers, there was probably more than one stud along the road. Or, if it was only one stud, it had plenty of land for grazing. Supposedly it was the famous Hemel 'n Aarde Stud which had many winners to its name. Leaving the green countryside we rejoined road N2.

As we had seen previously when driving on a motorway, in many areas the road was cutting right through the middle of settlements. Neither bridge nor tunnel connected the cut-off sections on either side of the highway. Instead, narrow tracks were heading to the road on both sides, from where people crossed the road through the fast moving traffic. Often enough they not even hurried across the road but walked at a gentle pace in spite of cars approaching at a speed of 110km/h.

A spicy choice

We reached Swellendam during an afternoon downpour. The town was named after Hendrik Swellengrebel and his wife Helena Willemina ten Damme. Between 1739 and 1751 Swellengrebel was governor of the Cape, the only VOC governor who was actually born in the Cape. His early tenure was dominated by a violent conflict between the Company, white farmers and Khoi tribes many of whom were killed.

Nestling at the foot of the Langeberg Mountains, the small town had been founded in 1745 by the Dutch East India Company as a trading and control post. It is the fourth oldest European town in South Africa. The arable land around the settlement was, and still is, extensively used. The landdrost, a representative of the governor, had been stationed there to keep an eye on unruly settlers. His residency and office, the Drostdy, was one of the earliest buildings still existing, it had been turned into a museum. The place was closed when we were in town.

A few churches and some well kept private residences would have made a short walk through the village worthwhile. But not in the driving rain. There were no other visitors, in fact we did not see a single person. In view of the heavy downpour, everybody had taken refuge indoors.

We popped into a butcher's shop on Voortrek Street where we were the only customers. They were selling what we loved best: locally made boerewors and biltong. The latter being fillet of meat, either dried, salted, spiced and cut into stripes or grated. The meat used was venison, beef, mutton or ostrich. Boerewors was a spiced sausage for barbecue or pan. Another type was droewors, also a dried spicy sausage. A large selection, and which one should we take?

We had a difficult decision to make. In order to help us make up our minds, the owner served us a few samples to taste and choose, and we were not reluctant to oblige. Faced with the enticing Boer specialities, we were unable, or unwilling actually, to make a choice. To resolve the dilemma, we bought a good quantity of each. That delighted the shop assistants whose selling strategy had paid off, and it also pleased us very much. Considering the uninspiring weather, this transaction brightened up the afternoon, making both sides happy. Loaded with heavy carrier bags, we bought further essentials at a grocer's next door. To compensate for the rain, strawberries were acquired for dessert.

Antelopes in the rain

Bontebok National Park was 6km from Swellendam. It was the day's destination. The park has been devoted to the preservation of the rare and captivating antelopes called bontebok. Peter could not wait to see them.

Once they roamed a much wider area in large numbers. By the end of the 18th century their situation had become endangered as the secretary to the first British governor at the Cape reports: "Few antelopes, except the Reebok, Steenbok, and Duyker, are now remaining in the district of Zwellendam. Formerly, the Bontebok [...] was almost as numerous near the Drosdy."[46] By 1840 they had been reduced to the verge of extinction, just 300 animals were left in the region at the end of the 19th century, by 1930 only 30 of them.

First established at a different location in 1931, an antelope sanctuary was moved to the present area in the 1950s

---

[46] John Barrow, An account of travels into the interior of southern Africa, I, p350.

and designated a national park in 1962 with 61 bonteboks; at present about 1,500 lived within the boundaries
of the park. Not only bonteboks inhabited the park but
also duiker, steenbok, ribbok, grysbok, mongoose, caracal,
porcupines, foxes, dassies, zebras, and jackals. Because of
the large variety of wildlife and plants Peter had put the
park on the itinerary.

Singed socks and dripping boots

We were greeted by a group of grey ribboks, 'my welcome
committee' as the lady at the reception desk said. We were
expected, since we had made a reservation from Britain by
phone. No one else was staying overnight, and there were
no other visitors in the park at the time.

Our lodgings were close to the Breede River, about
12km from the entrance. We slowly drove along the winding dirt road which runs as a one-way system through the
park, a pan of open grasslands with low fringes and the
Langeberg Mountains in the background.

A small family of four hartebeest was looking at the
passing car with curiosity. Grey duikers and a few bonteboks could be seen in the distance. Feeding on leaves,
flowers and pods, the resident antelopes found the vegetation much to their liking.

The camp was situated on a bend of the river. It offered
basic accommodation in a fully furnished caravan and an
adjacent wooden anteroom fixed to it, with an iron bed,
a few chairs, and a fridge. This arrangement was called
a chalavan. Peter had booked it because he was curious
what exactly it was. Bathrooms and showers were in a
separate building. Reassuringly, there was an emergency
phone connecting to the manager's cottage. Heating there
was none.

Although it was still raining, we decided to take a look at our surroundings before nightfall. There were two walking trails from the camp, both of which we checked out. One led to the Aloe Hills above the river. We did not go far because it was wet and slippery, as could be expected. The second path on the other side of the camp ran through dense and tall grasses and under bushes and small trees. We walked as far as a small creek then went back as the narrow track was too muddy. The constant rain did not encourage further exploration.

Our leather walking boots were well and truly soaked, they were squeaking. Nicely drenched we got back into the chalavan which was dry but not warm. The temperature outside was not much above 10°C, inside it was about the same. Luckily, the rain did not find its way through the roof, and we were gradually drying up.

Peter and Greg prepared dinner on a small cooker in the caravan section, the driver was excused from any work after a day at the steering wheel. Given the rudimentary kitchen equipment, the two chefs managed to serve a gourmet meal of boerewors, fried tomatoes with cheese and bread, crowned by a bowl of sweet straws topped up with a white cloud of whipped cream. This we considered a well deserved heavenly treat.

With his pyrotechnic skills Greg was able to get a reluctant gas lamp going, generating a vague feeling of comfort and some warmth. Considering the circumstances we felt very civilized. Peter's attempts at drying his dripping socks closest to the source of the heat resulted in a revolting smell of roasted wet wool, counterbalancing the spicysweet bouquet of our dinner.

Thanks to a generous supply of woollen blankets, four of those for me, we all were warm and slept soundly until the wake up calls of noisy birds early next morning.

'Why such a bloody racket at this hour', I yelled at them.

'This is our early bird routine, and we will not be stopped by your screaming at us.' With this pompous reply they happily continued being a nuisance.

'But not mine, and you could have some consideration for your guests', I hissed back. And on they chirped with even more enthusiasm.

Confronted with such unexpected gift of eloquence before I was ready to face the day, unsettled me somewhat. Cursing, I pealed off the layers of heavy wraps and shouted for someone to bring a cup of strong tea please. But none for the chorus outside.

Mossy fairies, chocolate boks

It was not raining yet, so we decided to take another hike. We cleared our quarters, packed the car and rebuked the birds, and walked up Aloe Hills on the same trail we had turned back on the previous day.

The grass was still, or again, covered in rain drops. Not long after we set off, the drizzle started once more. Our drenched walking gear was getting even more saturated than it already was. Yet, undaunted, we walked on.

As this was an area of high rainfall, mosses profusely covered the tree trunks, and strands were hanging suspended from branches high up behind a veil of humidity. It was like walking through an enchanted forest with fairies peeping from behind the green curtains.

We observed the comings and goings in a colony of busy weaver birds, their neatly-woven nests dangling precariously on the tips of long branches. In the reeds, in the shallows of the river, a community of colourful birds had taken up residence. The plumage was orange and black, their faces were orange-red. A malachite sunbird, a glossy bright green bird with a long blue tail, was also going about its daily tasks.

Many tall aloes were growing in the Breede River area, they could be seen everywhere. One such specimen was gracing the space in front of our luxurious abode. The multi-stemmed aloe had a cluttered look about it. Robust and majestic, the plant with its greenish fleshy leaves dominated the not very grassy area. It was quite impressive.

Thoroughly soaked we arrived back at the car. We slipped into dry clothes and dry spare shoes and made our way to the exit. The road back to the front desk was the remaining part of the one-way loop along the side of the pan.

Frequently stopping and taking our time, we enjoyed the beautifully coloured countryside. The vegetation showed a rich diversity. Areas of low shrubs, pink flowers, red blossoms, yellow patches, grasses, ericaceae. Small plants, fine leaves, small flowers: that was the fynbos. Requiring sandy soil poor in nutrients, the region offered the right conditions for the species to thrive.

And of course there were plenty of bonteboks. They allowed us to observe them at close range in small and larger groups. Their coats were of a mellow brown like my favourite Belgian chocolate. They were medium sized antelopes with a wide white patch in the face from their horns down to the nostrils. The bellies were white, the legs down from the joints were white, and there was a big white patch at the root of the dark tail.

A duiker ducking in the grass was doing his best not to be discovered. The tiny antelope, just about 50cm tall at the shoulder and weighing not more than 20kg, with a greyish-reddish coat was nearly invisible among the vegetation. Standing rigid and staring at us with suspicion for a moment, he did not trust us one bit and bolted away.

Since we were driving very slowly with long stops in order to observe or to take pictures, it took one and a half hours to cover the short distance of 7km to reception.

A quick bite for lunch in the shape of addictive biltong, and we were on the N2 in an easterly direction, passing a number of small farming towns.

Our next destination was one that Greg had put on the list of things to do, see or visit.

The hazards of sailing in times past

Mossel Bay was a small fishing and farming town which had been a busy little harbour of the Dutch. With the discovery of offshore gas fields the port mainly serves the oil and gas industry. A destination for beach tourists, the place was interesting to us for a different reason.

Greg, a dedicated yachtsman with a couple of sailing trips around the Bahamas under his belt, wanted to go to the Bartholomeu Dias Museum.

On the deck of Dias' ship

The main attraction was a replica of the explorer's vessel, used on his voyage at the end of the 15th century. With a small fleet of three ships Dias had left Lisbon in August 1487, charged with finding a trade route to India. He had been sent out by King Joao II to probe Portuguese prospects of breaking into the spice trade, which at that time was dominated by Venetian and Arab merchants. He was also to establish relations with Indian princes. In February 1488, the expedition replenished their water supplies in the bay, now called Mossel Bay. They sailed back to Portugal after a few more weeks further along the coast. He arrived at his home port in December of that year.

Dias' ship was a caravel, a trading vessel of 23.5m length and a maximum width of 6.60m. This type of two-masted sailing ship was used by the Spanish and Portuguese in the 15th and 16th century. Celebrating his voyage, 500 years later, a faithful copy of Dias' ship had been sailed from Portugal to Mossel Bay. This time however, for safety reasons, the reproduction was equipped with state-of-the-art technology. In contrast to the explorer's six months passage, the trip of 1987 took only three months. This was the ship we were inspecting.

Greg, most knowledgeable about everything concerning ships and navigation, could not help himself explaining every detail of the very vessel. At least two helmsmen below deck handled the heavy tiller, a wooden or iron bar fitted to the rudder in order to steer the ship by moving it from side to side. Their instructions, as to which way to push or pull, were shouted down to them from the poopdeck via one or two hierarchical levels. They could not see anything as they were inside the hull. Amazing to think how a boat of such a small size was able to withstand ferocious ocean waves and long arduous voyages. The crew must have been immensely tough and hardened sailors.

Nine years after Dias, Vasco da Gama put in with his fleet of four ships and 170 men at about the same spot on the African coast. He, however, continued to the East and made contact with local rulers in India. With three ships and 80 men, the first Portuguese fleet that had made it to India returned to Lisbon in July 1499.

In May 1500, together with over 350 sailors out of a crew of 1,500 and four ships, Bartholomeu Dias perished when his ship sank in a savage storm in the Atlantic off the coast of the Cape during Portugal's second successful expedition to India, on the occasion of which Brazil was discovered. Dias was in command of one of the thirteen ships of the well-armed fleet which was sent out by King Manuel I and headed by the nobleman Pedro Álvarez Cabral.

A few years after I was on Dias's vessel so to speak, I stood at the famous spot near Lisbon where the navigators and their achievements were commemorated. The Torre de Belem on the shore of the river Tejo, as part of a defence system, had been erected after Dias' and da Gama's first expeditions. In the Maritime Museum close-by, models of naval and merchant ships were on display showcasing Portugal's discoveries and explorations through the centuries. In the entrance hall, visitors were welcomed by a statue of Infante Dom Henrique, son of King Joao I, who had been the driving force in the country's quest in the first half of the 15th century. The navigators he had sent out explored the West coast of Africa, paving the way for subsequent expeditions like those of Dias and da Gama.

Maritime disasters

A section of the museum was devoted to the countless tragedies in the off-shore waters around the Cape and farther to the east. Instructive graphics illustrated the dangers to shipping in previous centuries and pointed out the locations of shipwrecks along the coast. Some ships went down on their way to India, others on their homeward voyage. Some were never found, others centuries later. Often enough it was well known exactly where and when which ship had disappeared.

The Portuguese ship *Sao Joao*, on its way back home, sunk in 1552 off Natal and was discovered 430 years later. The *Sacramento*, also returning to Portugal from Goa, in 1647 perished in Algoa Bay and was found in 1977. Two Dutch Indiamen were lost near Cape Town on the outward voyage around 1700, to be located more than 250 years later. The *Doddington* of the British East India Company, bound for India in 1755, carrying cannons and soldiers for the British India Army as well as large amounts of silver, came to grief on one of the islands off Port Elizabeth. She was found in 1977 and subsequently salvaged. There were so many more.

If it was not known where a ship had foundered, it was sometimes possible to attribute finds of cargo like pieces of China to a particular wreck from its pattern, size, or make. Such discoveries often established the location or identification of a sunken vessel.

Deficient marine charts

Ships could be blown off course by the force of strong winds and currents, or by raging seas and battered to pieces on rocks. But often enough it was a lack of proper information or useful instruments. Incorrect hydrographic maps of previous times overlayed with correct modern ones illustrated plainly how the wrong coastlines shown on those maps caused the ships' doom. In many places the old charts did not indicate the true line of the coast and its hazards, like treacherous sandbanks or perilous rocks lurking beneath the surface, or the correct depth of water.

A ship's safety was also at risk on account of the wrong interpretation of charts, were there any. A report in *The Oriental Navigator*, sailing instructions for the benefit of all shipping in the early 1800s, noted how ships "have unexpectedly fallen in with many dangerous shoals; erroneously supposing, that the vacant space in the charts indicated that part to be free from danger, instead of being unexplored." The available charts and specifications had to be updated on a regular basis to improve each ship's safety and minimize the risks. Captain Robert Butler, on his way to China after having passed the Cape of Good Hope, noted in his report how "the want of correct charts on board, and of accurate information respecting the track I intended to follow, occasioned me to pay the utmost attention to all the observations I made [...] and loosing no opportunity of ascertaining our specific situation each moon by meridional double altitudes and lunar observations, day and night."[47]

In earlier times sailing charts were secret documents, to be kept hidden from rival companies and countries for reasons of commercial advantage or political strategy. Often, they were just manuscripts which were used together with the log that contained information on coastlines, rocks, islands, places to seek shelter. As the sunken ships proved, the early charts had their limitations, their inaccuracies leading to loss of men, cargo and ships.

Inadequate nautical aids

The great number of shipwrecks along the South African coast, and elsewhere, was not only owing to the want of correctly chartered routes, but also to non-satisfactory navigational aids. The displays in the museum told of the implications and consequences to the ships and their crews of not yet having adequate scientific and nautical instruments. Only in the second half of the 18th century, with the invention of John Harrison's chronometer, did it become possible to precisely determine the location of a ship

---

[47]p503, p615. On charts and cartographers see Fell and Tooley.

by latitude and longitude. Not knowing for certain the exact position of their vessels and relying on estimates, the master of one of the ships in the fragmented fleet of Commodore George Anson, one night in April 1742, thought they were far out west of the South American coast safely on the open sea, when in reality they were short of crashing into its coastal rocks. Their near fatal error was rectified at the last minute.

The navigator had to determine the position of the ship at any one time and the course to be followed in order to arrive at the desired destination. The fate of the ship, her cargo and crew depended on his reckoning of the direction and distance travelled, the effects of winds and currents, errors of the log or compass, by taking reference to known objects or coastlines or by astronomical observations of the sun, moon, planets or stars. However, even with some aids available things did not always go to plan. On its way to the Cape, in summer 1653, a ship from Holland had taken more than eight months, the time usually needed to get as far as Batavia. The fact that the voyage had lasted so much longer than it was supposed to was due to an error of an important navigational instrument: "They had been misled by variations of the compass."[48] At least, the vessel was only late by a few weeks and not wrecked as so many others were.

Poor seafaring expertise

The human factor also added to the likelihood of disasters happening. Inadequate experience and flawed seamanship contributed to the wrecking of ships as well as lack of leadership and discipline. Manning the ships with mariners experienced in oceanic sailing was challenging. As most

---

[48]Van Riebeeck's Journal, I, p158.

countries were short of seamen, the limited number of seasoned sailors available was redressed by recruiting foreign
or unskilled manpower. At times, peasants ended up as
crew without receiving any training at all. They had been
hired by agents and came straight off their farms, or they
had just taken their chance at sea. The urban poor, in time
of need, were also enrolled. Living and working conditions
on board were hard. Low morale, disobedience within the
ranks as well as disciplinary measures like corporal punishment meted out by the officers could unsettle an underfed
and underpaid crew and threaten the safety of the vessel.

Even the commanders of a fleet were not always experienced. Pedro Álvarez Cabral was appointed as commander-
in-chief of the Portuguese fleet sailing for India in 1500,
even though he did not have any maritime experience but
personal connections. In due time, most naval powers recognized that training for crews, in particular the education
of officers, was necessary. In 1701 the Søe Cadet Com-
pani was established in Copenhagen, in 1717 the Academia
de Guardias Marinas in Cádiz, in 1732 the Royal Naval
Academy at Portsmouth Dockyards, in 1782 the Compan-
hia dos Guardas-Marinhas in Porto, and in 1816 the Collège
de la Marine in Angoulême.

The quality of shipbuilding

Besides the capabilities of the sailors and officers, one significant aspect of a voyage also contributed to its success
or failure: the vessel itself. Its dimensions, structure, en-
durance, durability, stability, strength and carrying capacity as well as the quality of the timber and the workman-
ship at the shipbuilding yards were of paramount importance. Its seaworthiness, manoeuvrability and sailing qualities were interrelated.

The *Vasa* is a well-documented case in point. The warship of King Gustav Adolf II sank in 1628 in Stockholm harbour with the loss of many lives just shortly after its launch. It had been toppled by a gust of wind within the shelter of the port. Wrong proportions with a high centre of gravity are said to have caused instability of the vessel and its capsize as a consequence. Some time after my visit to Mossel Bay, I stood near that magnificent ship within its very own museum. Here it had been exhibited since 1990 after being found in 1956, raised in 1961, preserved and reconstructed for decades. Many resplendent vessels like the Swedish ship were lost at sea, as the material in the Dias museum amply testified.

Further exhibits were graphics, illustrations and explanations about explorations, trade routes and trade relations across the world as well as relevant maps and charts. Everything was greatly interesting and deserved more attention, and I would have liked to study this section of the museum in more detail.

As we had a booking further along the road, we could not spend more time at the museum. We had to move on.

A string of historic towns

Later in the afternoon we arrived at George Tourist Resort where a spacious brick cottage had been booked for one night. The place was not busy but a note at check-in implied that it was a very lively destination: "Please have respect for your neighbours. Please keep noise levels to a reasonable limit in order not to annoy other guests." I was wondering what was usually going on here.

Next morning we drove into town where Peter was scheduled to give a lecture at Hurteria College, a campus of Nelson Mandela Metropolitan University in Port Elizabeth.

Grown out of a forestry college, the institution in George today has come to cover wood technology, forestry and natural resource management as well as business and information technology.

While Peter was dispensing words of wisdom, Greg and I took a short walk around the nearest part of the town. It had been established in late 18th century by the Dutch East India Company, taking advantage of the rich supply of timber. Named after George III, at the time King of the United Kingdom of Great Britain, it was proclaimed the town of George in 1811. Today, it is a substantial place with many attractions.

Completed in 1842, the Dutch Reformed Church at the corner of Courteney Straat and Kerk Straat was an impressive building set in its own large garden. Using slave labour it had taken twelve years to build. The interior was decorated with fine dark wood; made from yellowwood and stinkwood, the large pulpit was exquisite. It was a wonderful place to contemplate and reflect.

The stereo system in the church played Johann Sebastian Bach's *Brandenburg Concertos*. Written in 1721, the six concerti grossi are among my favourite pieces of Baroque music. The only visitors, we enjoyed the private concert immensely.

Once there were elephants and trees

The next port of call was Knysna. There we were booked into a hotel exuding an air of cool elegance. It was at the Quays right at the marina. We had two bright and spacious rooms next to each other, each with a balcony which was disgraced by our wet boots for the next twenty-four hours.

From the second floor we had a view over the harbour and across the lagoon. There were boats of all shapes, sizes and nationalities. Almost at our feet in front of our rooms, a number of stylish luxury yachts and large catamarans were moored. There was even a trimaran with a very tall mast resembling the tailfin of an aircraft, an impressive sight. This kind of double- or triple-hulled type of vessel offers great stability and great speed. A paradise for yachtsman Greg, himself owner of a catamaran. He explained all dimensions of boating to us from skiffs to standard sailing boats to the ocean-going cats ploughing the seas. Both brothers had travelled in kajaks among drift ice in the fjords of Greenland. My own experience on the Mediterranean coast, also on a cat, was too insignificant to mention.

Close to the hotel was a small railway station which we passed just at the right time. The tourist attraction of the place was about to arrive: the steam train running between George and Knysna. With a lot of noise it pulled in, whistling and puffing. Much to Greg the engineer's delight, who pointed out all the features of the locomotive: where the water was filled in from above, where the coal was stored, where the ashpan was and the location of the whistle and the blast pipe as well as the workings of the running gear. He happily obliged to answer any questions anyone of the attending crowd threw at him about the technical details of this feat of engineering.

We went walkabout around the small town. A crowded bus station right in the centre held our attention for a considerable time. It was frequented by local people only. Many of the shops were about to close for the day, so people were waiting for their trip home into the surrounding villages and settlements. A vast number of honking minibuses was leaving, each packed beyond capacity with people and their heavy shopping bags. Pouring out fumes and whirling up dust, the overloaded vans with tyres almost flat seemed on the verge of collapsing.

A few hundred years ago, the town had been an important place for timber exports and shipbuilding. After 1810, a large area of the forest had been cut down to supply the Royal Navy with material for their vessels. When quartz was discovered in the 1870s and gold in the 1880s, more of the forest was axed to make way for roads. Logging, fires, erosion, as well as settlements and farm expansions destroyed much of the ancient woods. The exploitation of the forest caused severe habitat degradation and loss of animals. Still, there are areas left said to be the largest indigenous forest in the country.

Once, there had been many elephants in the forests around Knysna, in the foothills of the mountain range and further along the wooded regions of the coast. Already in the 18th century their numbers had been reduced by the white colonists. Almost all of those that had remained were killed in the 1920s, mainly by the adventurer and big-game hunter Major Philip Jacobus Pretorius, for science and for sports, authorized by the government. How many are left there today, cannot be established with any reliable certainty.

A study of wildlife researcher Gareth Patterson and a team of forest guards suggests that, as of 2011, there appeared to be around nine elephants. He narrates his seven years of fieldwork from 2001 onwards and discusses the findings in his captivating account *The Secret Elephants*. Equalling spellbinding is the book *Elephantoms* by naturalist Lyall Watson, who marvels at the spiritual power of the animals and the mysteries of their lives around the dense depth of the impenetrable forest.

The following morning we drove to the Heads, the narrow separating Knysna lagoon from the Indian Ocean. Passing a golf course, a small side road was running through marshland into a residential area. Luckily tour busses were not able to navigate the road. It became steep and went up right to the cliffs. The view from up there was fantastic. A couple of homes with large wooden decks clung on to the edge, enjoying the panorama every day.

Far down, the surf thundered against the rocks.

Whales and dassies

At noon we were parked at Storms River in the Tsitsikamma National Park. It was windy, 25°C, with bright sunshine and a strong surf.

We walked the mondwandelpad or mouth trail to the river. From the shaded board walk the view over the rocks and surf was magnificent. We took our time. Many stinkwood trees were growing on the steep slope next to the trail, birds were flying along. We arrived at the suspension bridge across the water. Dassies were basking in the sunshine on huge boulders at the river's mouth. Quite a number of people had gathered here, entering the bridge for a few metres, taking pictures, debating whether to go on or not, deciding not to, instead taking more selfies with the hyraxes looking on. It was just like on Table Mountain.

While I did not wish to walk on that bridge, the two brothers continued the trail across the creek and up the hill on the far side to a viewpoint overlooking the ocean. They were rewarded for their short climb by the presence of a whale close to the shore. Several varieties of proteas satisfied their interest in the local flora. Since no one else went further than the bridge, they had the lookout all to themselves.

I decided not to wait at the bridge for their return; it was too crowded for me. Slowly, I ambled back the path we had come, there did not seem to be an alternative route. I very much enjoyed my walk through the forest and the view of the ocean through the trees on my left. The sea was rough and roared, the waves came rolling in, pounding the rocky shore.

Starting from the camp area, we took the second walk. Unlike the first track which mainly ran along the water, the loeriewandelpad or loerie trail led up into the hills. Quite steep in places, the path ran among green shrubs and bushes.

We came to a lookout platform from where we watched a whale slowly cruise the waters, probably the same Greg and Peter had seen earlier. It was just arching its back to commence a deep dive and disappeared.

The powerful breakers of the Indian Ocean were roaring. The sun's rays penetrated our clothing. The distant horizon seemed to be endless.

On the way back down, we spotted a plant we had not noticed on the way up.

Eye-catching pops of colour in the lush dense foliage grabbed our attention. Sparkling blooms of a strikingly vibrant reddish-orange colour brightened the surrounding greenery. They were flashes glowing among the shrubs, almost inflamed by the sunshine. Producing sugary nectar at the base of its elongated flowers, the stunning plant attracts birds and insects. I am certain it was a Watsonia tabularis of the iris family, named in honour of 18th century naturalist, botanist and scientist Sir William Watson, FRS.

Rather than again jump into the car, we would have preferred to stay at Storms River, but had to leave for Port Elizabeth. However, accommodation was already booked right here for an overnight stay in the following week on our return trip back to Cape Town.

Around the Eastern Cape

A further 200km, and we arrived at Port Elizabeth after dark. While refuelling, we were given directions to the guest house we had been booked in by the university: "Turn right at the third robot". A new and amusing term to us for a traffic light, which in fact is, as an artificial intelligence powered signal, a kind of robot.

Next morning Peter was scheduled to give a lecture at the Nelson Mandela Metropolitan University. His host came to the lodge to welcome us and walk us to the campus. The university, a large higher education institution, had a diverse student population from many countries and ethnic backgrounds. While Peter was giving his talk, Greg and I explored the buildings and facilities of the university. Rejoining our host and his guest, we walked over to the Faculty Club to have lunch.

In the afternoon, we had a little walk in town. It was founded in 1820 when the Cape was British and, like other places, named after a person. In this case, after Elizabeth the prematurely deceased wife of the Governor Rufane Donkin. At that time, arrivals from Britain were encouraged to settle the frontier area and defend the eastern region of the British territory against the Xhosa.

In parts, we followed the Heritage Trail, which connected a few historic spots like the first terraced house to the ruins of Fort Frederick. Overlooking the Baakens River, the fortifications were built in 1799 to defend the harbour below against a potential attack by the French but abandoned after seventy years. Settlers' Park was a public park sloping down to the river. Its cultivated and natural gardens were a good place to watch birds and dassies.

Today, the port of Port Elizabeth is as important as it was then, only on a bigger scale. Car manufacturers like Ford, General Motors or Volkswagen have large plants in the city. Tourism also brings in a lot of revenue.

We left Port Elizabeth at 8am for the most interesting part of our southern adventures. Our destinations for the day were two national parks, Addo Elephant National Park and Mountain Zebra National Park. In the first we spent a few hours, in the second we stayed a couple of days.

Two perfect excuses for travelling to South Africa.

Sanctuary for the giants

Our first port of call was situated in the Sundays River valley at the Zuurberg Mountain range. An hour's drive on the R335, and we arrived at Addo Elephant National Park. Established in the 1930s, this park was mainly devoted to preserving the elephants of the Eastern Cape. Before that initiative was introduced, they had been under serious threat from humans, who considered them a menace. They were almost wiped out by poachers and farmers, and by one ivory hunter in particular.

From destruction to safety

In the 1920s, Major Philip Jacobus Pretorius, as in Knysna, had been commissioned by the authorities to reduce the existing herds in the area. Local tribes and colonial settlers had pushed more and more into the elephants' territory who, in return, raided their fields, having been deprived of their roaming and grazing opportunities. The confrontation between humans and animals was solved by the hunter's double-barrelled rifle. The elephants were no match for the major's bullets, about 120 of them were destroyed within ten months; around a dozen animals survived the carnage. After this act of wholesale slaughter, a park was established about ten years later. Today, it is the third largest national park in South Africa.

In 1931, Harold Trollope, previously ranger at Kruger National Park, was appointed the first warden of Addo. It was not only the elephants he needed to preserve but also the Cape buffalos who were poached at night at the waterholes; his focus, however, was on the grey pachyderm. Panicked and frightened by what had been done to their herds, the remaining elephants had become vengeful and aggressive. The warden and his field rangers had a dangerous task, as they had to drive the animals into the area destined to be the new park and their refuge. The elephants often broke out, but with his bush skills and fine-tuned hunter's instincts Trollope succeeded in persuading them that this was their new home. To his utter dismay, he had to kill at least two when they attacked his men. Three years later, the herd had accepted their safe haven and gradually began to settle and calm down. There were about fourteen elephants and thirty buffalos.

But in 1968 all was not well. One particular elephant had not forgotten what had been done to his ancestors. Hapoor, a very strong bull, who had dominated the area for a quarter of a century, had never stopped hating humans. Given the long memories within elephant families he had every reason for his abhorrence of men, in particular those with a gun. The awful irony is that the same happened to him almost fifty years after Pretorius' shots.

Today, about 600 elephants are living in the park and thriving. With numbers amounting to 400 animals, the buffalos are also doing fine.

Many other animals were there too

There were still areas in the reserve, where the vegetation was a jungle with spiky scrub of the green needle-bush and spekboom trees several metres high. One could easily imagine how the warden and his rangers had cut their way through the impenetrable thicket of tangled leaves, sharp spines, sticky berries and toxic latex in their search for the elusive massive animals.

Only a few cars were on the dirt roads through the undulating terrain. Winding our way along, we saw tall aloes and euphorbias and a number of flowering plants. In the semi-arid to arid area, there was a wide diversity of plants from trees and shrubs to succulents and grasses. We, however, were more interested in the fauna than the flora.

The elephants had plenty of company: buffalos, hyenas, warthogs, hartebeest, zebras, caracals, baboons and many more. A variety of birds and reptiles could also be found. Some of them we saw.

A small group of very tall antelopes came to a halt when they became aware of us. They were eland, with a pale yellowish-brown almost sand-coloured coat with around fifteen white vertical stripes. Because of a vague similarity to the Nordic creature, the Dutch had named it after the elk and called it eland. Standing 150-170cm tall at the shoulder and weighing between 460 and 700kg, these were one of the largest of the African antelopes. Spiralled at the base, their 65cm long magnificent horns, which both sexes had, swept straight back. We had not encountered them before. Laurens von der Post admired them greatly: "He is a noble animal, an aristocrat. He is the greatest of the antelope, big and strong but also extremely gentle, never using his giant strength like a giant. He is beautiful to look at, and the life within him burns like a subtle flame in the colours of his coat."[49] Looking at the vehicle for a few minutes, they turned into a grove of trees threading their way through the foliage and out of sight. We saw them a few times during our tour around the park.

A herd of buffalos could not be bothered by our presence. Some noticed the car but looked on unconcerned. I wondered whether they had forgotten that many of their kind had been killed by settlers and poachers almost a hundred years ago. I hoped their memories were not as long as the elephants'.

---

[49]The heart of the hunter, p213.

A new threat has materialized albeit not a deadly one. Because the buffalo herds at Addo have no diseases, they are in demand as breeding-stock, and family groups have been auctioned off for years. They are not the only ones that have been captured and removed. However, as the animal population is growing and the park area has its limiting boundaries, the revenue generated by such sales is being used to acquire land for conservation.

Majestic secretary birds that had already impressed us in the Krugerpark were walking among some low shrubs. Several ostriches were also on a stroll. Tall birds, they often came in pairs, his feathers being mainly black, hers greyish brown. A tortoise made its way from a waterhole up a grassy slope, moving slowly through the green blades. It was probably the triumphant Kamba who had just fooled two giants into an unfair contest and boldly considered himself the winner, until they were going to find out.

But it was for the largest land animals that we had come to Addo.

Sharing a drink with the elephants

At Hapoor waterhole I parked the car, and we waited for things to happen. The pond was named in honour of the dangerous elephant bull killed in 1968.

About midday, the temperature was 26°C in bright sunshine. So it was highly likely that animals would come here to drink. Driving to the place we had seen a few grey blobs moving in the distance. We were not the only ones noticing several large elephant herds en route to the spot. Seven cars were facing the waterhole with great expectations, and so did we.

With the engine switched of, the vehicle was warming up, making us as thirsty as the elephants. In anticipation of their imminent arrival, we had a drink ourselves from the water bottles.

One elephant family not far away was making their way through the shrubs towards the water. The calves among them were playing with each other and rolling about in the grass. They were reprimanded by their mothers to stop the nonsense and encouraged to keep up. The herd appeared slightly nervous, rushing across the road to get to the water quickly. They were worried about their calves, not because of our presence but because of a lone elephant bull following them at a distance. They wanted to get out of his way as fast as possible. Therefore they did not stay longer than necessary at the waterhole. Finished with splashing and drinking, the herd hurried into the vegetation on the opposite slope. Melting with their environment, they vanished into the shrubs and were impossible to see.

While they disappeared, the feared huge bull arrived.

'What a magnificent beast!'

'He walks right into our car', one of us exclaimed.

'Why would he do that for, he would only laugh at our water supply,' came from the front passenger seat.

'He could empty the small lake in one slurp, one of his size usually drinks about 200 litres a day, that is 400 of our bottles.' A quick calculation emanated from the rear.

'In case he changes his mind, we better sit tight and don't move.' The responsible driver cautioned.

'He wouldn't, he is smart, and we will, we are also smart.'

In quick steps the large bull approached. Passing between two wide-spaced cars, he trotted by right in front of our vehicle. We froze. Towering, his enormous size was frightening, he could have bulldozed us without any effort. But that was not at all his intention, his eyes focussed on the pond. He paid us no attention at all, water was more important at this time of day. We relaxed. The elephant took a good long drink, then turned and passed along our car. We froze again. Without giving us a glance, he walked off into the greyish scrub, disappearing instantly. We relaxed again.

That excitement merited a few more gulps of cold water. It would have been just a sip for the elephant.

Meanwhile members of another herd began to arrive one by one. Hapoor waterhole seemed to be the main source of water for the elephants in this section of the park. In the times of conflict between farmers and elephants, the problem of sufficient water sources for agricultural use and animal consumption had been a pressing issue. Nowadays, there are a good number of boreholes, dams and water points at various locations in the park meeting the needs of all animals.

Not only true giants inhabited the Addo park, there were also tiny creatures, that were giants in their own right.

Beetles of consequence

Piles of fresh and steaming droppings could be seen at many places on the dirt road, left by elephants who had recently walked along. The small heaps would not be there for very long. A six-legged workforce was probably already on their way.

The most amazing creatures in the park were the dung beetles. Owing to the considerable population of elephants, huge quantities of excrements were being generated. Feeding mainly on the dung of elephants but also of other herbivores, they eat the nutritious parts of the undigested food. They also use the dung as breeding chambers, for which purpose the droppings of buffalos or antelopes are preferred. By rolling the mass into balls, they move them in acrobatic manoeuvres to a safe location. We saw such laborious operations and marvelled at the strength of the creatures, dislodging and moving something that was their own size and weight many times over.

Their industriousness cleaned up the roads, maintaining a healthy environment by speeding up decomposition and redistributing the plentiful dung. Their small size was counterbalanced by their significance for the eco-system.

While the numbers of dung beetles are decreasing in general, the Addo population is doing well, in fact it is the largest in South Africa. The park management was concerned for their welfare. Warning signs along the roads advised motorists to exercise particular care not to run over the tireless little fellows. Owing to their great importance, they had to be given right of way.

The unobtrusive presence of the giants, the assorted feathered population and the tiny chaps on the pachyderms' dung made us feel entirely unimportant. We as humans had no meaning in their daily lives, only in their preservation. At least at this national park.

We spent almost five hours here. Since the park is so large and there is so much to see, we experienced only a fraction of the wildlife and the various landscapes of Addo. An overnight stay in one of the camps ought to be on the itinerary for the next South African adventure.

Very happy with what we had seen in the morning, we were now looking forward to what we would see in the afternoon.

I pointed the car to the N10, heading up north to Cradock.

On the Karoo

Our destination was the Mountain Zebra National Park on the eastern edge of the Karoo about 200km away.

The N10 was new and apparently built to carry much traffic. The highway connects Port Elizabeth in the Eastern Cape with the Northern Cape province and the border with Namibia, a distance of roughly 1,000km. There were numerous lorries on the road, but in total there were not many vehicles. Again, we saw people walk on the shoulder quite unconcerned about cars or trucks.

The road meandered through the varied areas of hills and dents along the Karoo, the arid tablelands of semi-desert. The vast region with its rolling slopes and flatland basins had a sweeping aspect, which was broken by steep rises and rocky crests. There was a sameness to it, that might be considered boring. The various hues and shades of the muted colouring of the sand, rock and vegetation bestowed a serene beauty on the landscape.

We gazed out of the window appreciating what aeons, sun and wind had accomplished.

The area is several hundred million years old. Over time, thick layers of sediment have built up and accumulated into sandstone. Recording the earth's history and preserving reptiles and amphibians long gone, the Karoo attracts geologists and paleontologists to interpret their findings. The San who inhabited the Karoo before European intrusion left rich paintings of humans and animals in many of the caves.[50]

Because of meagre rainfall and regular dry spells, the vegetation consisted mostly of sparsely distributed drought-resistant scrub and succulents. Olive Schreiner, in the open-

---

[50]For the development of sand and sediment into rock, e.g. on the Karoo, see Welland, chapter 7.

ing paragraph of *The Story of an African Farm*, pays credit to the drought-adapted flora of the landscape: "The dry, sandy earth, with its coating of stunted karoo bushes a few inches high, the low hills that skirted the plain, the milkbushes with their long, finger-like leaves." Most plants like dwarf shrubs were specialists in adjusting to this particular kind of habitat.

The idea that any kind of agriculture would be able to thrive in this "wide, lonely plain" seems to be far-fetched; and yet, since the 19th century, there have been large sheep runs producing meat and wool for textile industries.

European settlers' efforts in the semi-desert

With white colonists spreading farther inland, they claimed more and more land that was already occupied. Khoi were pastoralists who needed large sways of land for grazing their livestock. San were hunters and gatherers who roamed wide areas in search of food. Clashes were inevitable. The region along the Fish River was first settled by the Boers in the 1770s and by the mid 1800s by British settlers. Promoted as a desirable region by the government, the colonists flocked into the districts, continuously ousting indigenous peoples in the process.

The unceasing demands of the settlers for land suitable for livestock grazing, particularly sheep, drove them to acquire even extremely dry land, at times at exorbitant prices. Some remained poor farmhands, others became wealthy landowners. They stocked their property as best they could, sunk wells by tapping the plentiful underground water and transformed the land. Managing their possessions well and investing with prudence, they made a success of their ambitions and of life in an alien environment. If affected by famine and drought or by plummeting returns, they were crippled by debt or total ruin. Expectations and aspirations of the inhabitants of those farms were often shattered and did not lead to prosperity but to disillusionment and failure, dejection and death as described in Schreiner's tale.

A hopeless Karoo farm of literary fame

Very far in the distance, the binoculars showed some kind of buildings. Was it perhaps one of those estates, that had been established in the 1840s and managed to survive in its inhospitable environment to the modern era? How did it operate, who lived there, what kind of existence was possible? The hard life on such a farm in the Karoo is told in *The Story of an African Farm*, published in 1883.

The bitter realities of the daily struggle and the often violent interaction between the members of the farm community mirror nature's challenges: "The weary flat of loose red sand, sparsely covered by dry karoo bushes, that cracked beneath the tread like tinder." The intense dryness of the land is aggravated by "the fierce sunlight, till the eye ached and blenched [...] two sunflowers [...] outstared by the sun, drooped their brazen faces to the sand."(p4) Even sun-loving flowers almost perish in the full blaze of the sun's blistering glare. Heat and exposure is one thing but lack of water and desiccation is another. Dried out by piercing temperatures and the burning sun, poor rains or none at all is even worse. "From end to end of the land the earth cried for water [...] the pitiless sky, that like the roof of some brazen oven arched overhead." The animals of the farm were dying, the dams retained no water, the plants were withering but "only the milk-bushes, like old hags, pointed their shrivelled fingers heavenwards, praying for the rain that never came." (p10)

Plants, animals and humans were barely holding on to life in the harsh environment. In spite of the sun being so hot and the land so dry, settlers were determined to make a living. Schreiner's narrative of owners, labourers, visitors, relatives, farmhands presents a group of white and indigenous people, almost all of whom are unhappy and trodden down by circumstances; the little happiness there was is ending in death. Though raising some amount of livestock like pigs, sheep and cattle, chicken and ostriches, no level of prosperity has been achieved. Isolated and disfunctioning, the farm of the depressing story is barely able to subsist.

Farm life on the Karoo, in the 19th century, as depicted by the author was harder than many of the frontier settlers could have imagined.

A small country town

Before arriving at Cradock on the banks of the Fish River, we passed the high mountains on our left and right, the Coetzeesberg Range and the Winterberg Chain.

The town was named after John Cradock, British governor of the Cape from 1811 to 1814. After recurring battles with the Xhosa whose land was taken, it had been founded in 1813 as a seat for the deputy landdrost Andries Stockenström to uphold the authority of the colonial government on the eastern fringes. He, however, tried to restrain the settlers from pushing into Xhosa lands. In vain.

Over time, the place has grown from a tiny outpost on the frontier serving as military base, trading post and mission station to a commercial centre for the farming district along the banks of the river. Today, Cradock seems to be more known for its proximity to the national park and the fact that the novelist once lived in the town than for its past significance.

Laid out in a grid system, it was easy to navigate the place. Actually, it appeared to be a pleasant little town that would have deserved a visit, in particular the history museum presenting the development of the region.

'Can we not at least have a short visit to see the building and the garden?'

'We cannot.'

'And the novelist's house?', attempting an objection.

'You want to meet the zebras, don't you?'

'Hm.'

And that was that. Instead of parking at the parsonage or at Olive Schreiner's house, both National Monuments, we got out of the car in front of a supermarket. Rather than looking at the implements or furniture the pioneers had used or at the personal items and books by the author (her most famous I already owned), I had to check out the shelves of a grocery store. We loaded the shopping basket to capacity with a good supply of provisions for the coming days in the bush, with biltong high on our list. Another stop at a petrol station, and we were on the R61 leading to the day's final destination.

We were off to the zebras.

Visiting the mountain zebras

In the 1930s, the distinctive zebra had been on the brink of extinction. With probably less than fifty animals left in the wild, it was decided to establish a reserve to preserve it. Harold Trollope, until 1935 warden of Addo and previously ranger in Kruger, recommended a region near Cradock. The mountainous area with rolling hills and rich grasslands was perfectly suited for them. In 1938 the Park Board bought a farm with five animals who soon disappeared. Over the following years, groups of zebras were given to the institution. Today, after many more land acquisitions over 600 animals are living in the park.

At the entrance gate to Mountain Zebra National Park, we were welcomed with a bright smile by the friendly gate staff, paid the entrance fee and rolled in. The wide grassy plain and its protecting mountains filled us with anticipation.

As any kind of speed would whirl up the dust, we crawled along the dirt road. With the engine switched off for a while, we sat in the middle of the wide valley. A very peaceful and quiet spot. The atmosphere late in the afternoon was tranquil, the temperature was still 22°C, the air balmy and warmed by the sun.

Scanning our surroundings, three binoculars did not pick out the animals we were after.

'Do you see anything?'

'Do you?'

'No one there.'

'Tomorrow we'll see them.'

Despite our efforts, only duiker, springbok and ostriches could be seen but no zebras, who, as we found out, know exactly how not to be seen. Since we moved so slowly and stopped occasionally, it took forty-five minutes to get to reception, a mere 10km or so away.

The restcamp was located on gentle slopes along one of the valleys, nineteen brick cottages with their own patios facing the open grassland between the hills vis-à-vis. We took possession of our temporary home and settled in. The cottage had three bedrooms, an open-plan kitchen, a large dining table. Enough space to spend a whole week, but we were booked for only two nights.

Dinner was prepared by the brilliant chefs, whereas I, as the one behind the wheel for hours, was advised to do nothing.

By way of rounding off the day, we took a stroll around the neighbourhood. We did not meet anyone; we were almost alone in the camp which suited us just fine. Only a few of the houses were occupied, so there were not many people and even fewer cars. A couple of lizards could be seen darting away. A perfect setting to spend our time.

Morning tea with dassies

After a good night's sleep in the quiet camp we woke up fairly early. There was no sound coming from anywhere, not even some irritating chirruping. Some yawning and stretching, and I got out of bed and tottered to the kitchen to find the all-important kettle and the equally important teapot. Next challenge was to locate the tea-caddy with our loose leaf Darjeeling, even more important.

'Where is the teaeaea?'

'I don't know.'

'No idea.'

That did not help one bit. Searching our luggage, I discovered it hidden inside a folded towel for protection. So, we were saved.

The best place to start the day was outside. Seated on deck-chairs with our mugs in one hand, binoculars or a GPS in the other, we watched the sun rise. A pot of freshly brewed hot strong tea first thing in the morning was vital for us, but not for our light-footed neighbours.

A variety of birds was coming and going, and a group of dassies occupied the thornbush right in front of the verandah. They kept rushing up and down the prickly branches, not taking much notice of our presence. How many there were we could not make out. They appeared to be a sizeable family. We had met their relatives on Table Mountain and at Storms River, so it was nice to meet another branch of their widespread clan. The fact that they were related to the hyrax communities further west and even to the mighty elephant, was of no meaning to them. Other things were on their mind. Perched high up on the top branches they were awaiting the sun and the warmth. They did not mind our company, but would not be enticed to enter into conversation with us.

Wishing our new friends a splendid day, we left for the morning's tour of discovery.

Told off by a wildebeest

While the camp was located on the slopes of a low hill, the animals were to be found on the mountains opposite. Our vehicle, the only one on the road, worked its way up a steep road. Every now and then we stopped at lookout points to enjoy the magnificent views over the camp and the valley below. The large open spaces and the high mountains in the distance were a stunning sight. Greg, well supplied with gadgets for every task imaginable, took a reading on his GPS: we were at an altitude of 1585m.

We arrived on Rooiplaat, a large and wide plateau overlooking the area of hills, valleys and peaks in the background. We were the only car to be seen. With the engine switched off we were parked on the track and observed the local animals.

We had seen wildebeest before in the Krugerpark, but not in such numbers and not at relatively close range. On the open land, there were no shrubs to hide, and they were more exposed. With occasional snorts and grunts, they made their presence felt so to speak. The antelopes were grazing their way contentedly across the flat, some on their own and most in groups. Some were munching away, others just stood looking on or snoozing, others sauntered about.

The herd did not move much, they stayed together in a far flung group.

One animal had separated from his mates and was perhaps 25m away from the car, grazing on his own. First he did not seem to mind us, but after a while thought otherwise. He was not happy about our continued presence, not making out what we were.

'Go away!', he grumbled at us, turning his head.

'We are not doing anything, just enjoying your company.'

'But I don't your's, so go away', he replied.

'I am sorry but we don't mean you any harm, it is just a pleasure meeting you.'

Politeness did not appease him.

'Not for me it isn't. So, clear off', he persisted.

His powers of articulation had not the desired effect. Move we did not. The position we sat in was too good to give up, as we had a perfect view across the plateau to watch proceedings. So we had to accept that he felt uneasy, but were sorry all the same.

He became restless and began walking back and forth contemplating whether to stay put or move on. He did not like the situation and decided to better walk away. Firing a few reproachful snorts at us, he trotted off turning his head in disgust every few steps. Obviously he felt better in close proximity to his family.

We stayed put and enjoyed just sitting there watching the large number of wildebeest. They moved further away, leisurely plucking a blade of grass here and there and with nothing in particular on their agenda. Our friend had caught up with his herd and hopefully felt better.

There were no other animals around, and nothing much was going on. Winds were blowing, the sun was shining, no other visitors in the vicinity, just one lonely car inching along in the far distance after some time. It was just us and the residents. Nothing exciting was happening, which was exciting enough for us.

After at least half an hour, the engine was started again. Driving along very very slowly, far off we saw ostriches and springboks. The flat area of low shrubs and grasslands was so peaceful that any kind of speed would have disturbed the harmonious atmosphere. We spent three hours to cover the 10km roundtrip on the endless plaat.

And where were the zebras?

Camouflage in stripes

And then we found them. On the Kranskop roundtrip we discovered not just one but several groups of mountain zebras. The area here was mainly dry, steep and mountainous, with a rich diversity of grass species. That was the terrain they liked best.

Their coats were effectively white with dark brown or nearly black stripes, continuing into a short mane that stood upright. Their bellies were white, their legs also showed fine dark stripes, and their noses were of a reddish-brown colour. Standing just under 130cm at the shoulder and weighing under 240kg, they were smaller in size and mass than the Burchell's zebra we had seen in Kruger National Park, but their ears were larger. They usually came in families of four or five with one stallion guarding two or three mares and their foals.

With long ears pricked, a group of four interrupted their feeding and looked at us from a few metres away. With curious stares they were probably wondering what we wanted but did not ask. So we did not tell them that we had travelled to the park to find out whether they were indeed the masters of deception they were said to be.

The quartet was standing in the open under a blue sky and could be readily seen. But most of the time, spotting the mountain zebras was remarkably difficult. It was almost impossible to distinguish the animals from their surroundings. With their striped coats perfectly matching the pale-brownish grass and the grey stones, they blended seamlessly into the bushes and the long grass. When standing motionless further away within some thicket or undergrowth in a shaded location, they became virtually invisible.

Even staring at the place where they most likely stood and looked at us, it was a challenge to identify what was the zebra and what was the shrub. When with some effort differentiating between the leaves, the rocks and the animals, they could be seen more or less clearly. Your mind had to remove the obscuring grass, your eyes then had to focus on the selected spot and look hard to make out their contours. The interplay of their coat's colouration and pattern with the shape of the varied vegetation created a confusing veil of illusion, fooling everyone into thinking the zebras were not there. Hiding in plain sight, so to say. So, they were not there when in fact they were. Apparently a case of trompe-l'oeil.

I recalled the words of wisdom given by a seasoned hunter to a novice to the bush: "When they don't move, an' you don't jus' know what they look like, you kin 'most walk atop o' them. You got ter kind o' shape 'em in yer eye, an' when you got that fixed you kin pick 'em up 'most anywhere!"[51] Lacking his trained eyes and long experience, we were not quite as successful as he was but still managed a few times to penetrate the bewildering curtain of grasses and twigs to spot the clever animals.

I suspect they were delighted, outwitting us in a sense. And we were pleased with ourselves managing to see them at all. Again we were struck with admiration for the inge-nious trick of nature of melting flora and fauna, which was meant to disguise the zebras' presence from their predators and deceive the hunters to live another day.

Long-tailed camp guards, hyenas on a handle

We crept further along the dirt road down to the valley floor. Large holes dug into numerous termite mounds spoke of the incessant efforts of hungry aardvarks. Since they were nocturnal creatures, we did not see any but did appreciate their digging work.

At the entrance to the camp, agile arboreal vervet mon-keys were jumping from one tree to the next. Black-faced with hands, toes and tail tips also of a charcoal colour, the grey-coated climbers were looking for something to eat and amuse them. Even with the windows closed, we heard their noisy chatter. On their high-up post, they were also watch-ing the traffic pass through their patch. Peering down on

---

[51] Jock of the Bushveld, p35-36.

us with curiosity, they took notice but did not care much. They simply waved us through.

In the afternoon we toured the Rooiplaat once more. Again, we spent time with a couple of wildebeest who, however, did not mind us. Our friend of the morning whose displeasure we had incurred might have gone to another part of the plain. He probably knew from experience that the same cars had a tendency to show up repeatedly.

The zebras also accepted our presence, not bothered that we appeared again. They stood among a couple of rocks within tall grass almost as high as them. As before, that made it a challenge to spot them. Moving the binoculars very slowly along the vegetation to where we suspected them to be, we discovered the group.

Our second round was just as spectacular and exciting as the first one. We spent just as long as in the morning. Being so close to the animals without any other visitors anywhere near, almost made us feel as having a personal connection with them.

Before going to the restaurant for dinner, I went into the little shop to see what it had to offer.

As at the Table Mountain station, I acquired a mug, this time with three of the local zebras looking on. The mugs collected over the years keep reminding me of a particular journey alluded to by their individual decoration. This one will recall our experience with those animals that were not easy to see.

Hand-crafted from wood, two salad server sets also ended up in my bag. I loved their handles. One featured a pair of red-dotted hyenas looking out for prey, the other two elephants collecting grass with their trunks. In order not to damage them, we seldom use them. I am not sure those animals in the wild are as well protected as the ones in our dining-room drawer.

Final spotting success

After two nights in that wonderful area we had to return to Port Elizabeth. Reluctant to leave, we spent as long among the animals as our agenda would allow. We felt, it was not long enough.

We drove up again almost as far as the Rooiplaat and down and into the valley of the Wilgersboom River. Buffalo were supposed to be in this part of the park but we did not see any of the 400 that are said to live there. The aardvarks had been busy again digging for termites.

At a small lake near the track, three ostriches were chasing one female that did not want to be followed. Not appreciating their attentions, she ran away with the trio in hot pursuit. The males, conscious of being the largest living birds on the planet, ignored her protestations and kept on harassing her. While they displayed this kind of aggressive behaviour, another group was much more civil. Nine of the huge birds were gathered at the water, pecking away at the short grass or loitering in the shallows. Some eyed the endeavours of their three mates, dismissing their antics with sneering glances.

They probably did not know they were the lucky ones. Raised commercially for their eggs and killed for their meat and their leather, farming ostriches in South Africa has been a profitable business for a long time. In the 18th and 19th century their feathers were considered a desirable fashion accessory, resulting in the birds nearly being wiped out. At that time, Oudtshoorn on the Karoo was a centre of feather production; today, there still are a number of ostrich farms. With more than half of world output in ostrich articles produced in South Africa, breeding the animals had been a thriving venture, until competition from China claimed part of the market and persistent droughts afflicted the farmers' exports and revenue. Notwithstanding reduced margins, ostriches are turned into shoes, wallets and handbags just like the crocodiles.[52]

After four hours, we moved across the plain toward the exit gate. Again, we scanned the horizon for animals. All three binoculars were at the ready. Greg spotted a further group of mountain zebras in the far distance on the slopes.

'Where? There is only a small pile of rocks.'

'Go further to the right.'

'Still don't see them.'

'Next to a group of bushes.'

'No one there.'

'Yes, they are.'

'No, they are not.'

'Try again.'

'There they are! Crafty buggers, hiding behind the foliage.'

And there they stood, all innocence. Merging with the shrubs and the stones, they were there, and they were not. Counting them was even more of a challenge than discovering them in the first place. We agreed, it was a family of five. They were probably amused about our efforts. Repeating the guessing game, we mastered the challenge a second group of four threw at us. They had no mind of

---

[52]Also in earlier times ostrich farming was a precarious business; it is described in some detail by the novelist Anthony Trollope, who travelled around the country in 1877 and describes his observations on an ostrich farm in *South Africa*, vol I, p110-114.

being observed and retreated into the shade, where they were obscured even more by leaves and twigs under a row of trees. With the assistance of a steady hand and good quality field glasses, we succeeded and said 'Got you'! with some satisfaction.

With mutual congratulations, we closed the mountain zebra chapter of our itinerary.

We crept along the gravel road on our way out as slowly as on our way in.

Conferencing near the beach

In the early evening we were back in Port Elizabeth. Peter was here for a conference and meetings with colleagues, Greg and I were his sidekicks without any duties. The event was our primary reason to travel to South Africa and a welcome pretext to visit places and animals.

Now we had to turn our minds to the serious problems in the world of technology and forget about dassies, zebras and wildebeest.

Happy hour

For the next couple of days we were booked into a stylish hotel right at the waterfront, next to the conference venue. The car was safely parked in the fenced-in guarded hotel compound.

We had two interconnecting stately suites comprising three large rooms with ocean view. Two generously sized bedrooms with ensuite bathrooms, an attractive lounge, and two kitchen sections were to be our base for the coming days. All three rooms had double doors to the seafront balconies, which ran along the whole length of the suites. The large windows commanded views out to the Indian Ocean stretching into the far distance. We could not have wished for a more splendid accommodation and location.

At our feet stretched Algoa Bay where, in 1488, the fleet of Bartholomieu Dias had anchored before turning back to Portugal. Having seen the replica of his ship a few days earlier, this was a fitting place to stay. The port in the distance was busy, cargo ships were being tugged in, berthed and unloaded. Their tonnage and size was Dias' vessel's many times over, but they probably had not as many crew.

A few of whales and dolphines were cruising in the bay. Near the shore, kitesurfers were harnessing the winds, jumping and flying over the powerful surf. About six heroes were braving the elements.

We preferred dry land, in particular the hotel's verandah, overlooking the bay and not frequented by other patrons while we were there. The happy hour invitation by the manager helped to swing our thoughts from the creatures of the African bush and waters to the up-coming event.

The next two days were occupied by the conference and its social obligations. Peter spent much of his time in the meeting rooms, listening, discussing and giving talks. His entourage joined him for the reception and the conference dinner. Greg and I also attended some of the talks and Peter's lecture. For his troubles, he was presented with a wooden elephant. Since we had just been to Addo it was a truly appropriate present indeed. Hopefully, the carved animal from the savannah did not mind too much being airlifted to the northern hemisphere and placed among books and not among bushes.

When the conference was adjourned, Peter returned from an expedition to a nearby wine shop, triumphant with four bottles of estate wine from the Hamilton Russell and Meerlust wineries.

Back to where we set out

We started our drive back west. In two days' time we had to be at Cape Town airport.

On this day we only went as far as Storms River. Before we got to the National Park again we passed through large open spaces and some wooded areas. The impenetrable forests had been cut down long ago. In the 1860s and 1870s the indigenous trees had fallen victim to the axes of the roads department, whose road engineer Thomas Charles John Bain was commissioned to construct many new roads and mountain passes to open up the hinterland to traffic and commerce.

Brazen toll collectors

Slowly approaching the Tsitsikamma tollgate, we were inspected by two baboons. The car windows were still shut, as we had not expected to pay our fee to a primate vanguard. They were dismayed, as closed windows did not promise any gains. We could not drive on, since they jumped onto the car and placed themselves on the bonnet. Hoping for the odd chance, that maybe there was still something to get, they tried a proven method.

The smaller of the two moved to the windscreen, sat down right in front of me and intimidatingly stared at me, drilling his eyes into mine. That menacing closeness I did not like very much.

'You want to do the driving?', I crossly asked through the glass in a not very polite manner, feeling threatened by his unrelenting gaze.

He did not, having no valid licence. Accepting that fact, he kept on staring me down. I sat back into my seat. Gradually however, it dawned on him that this was a futile exercise, and he retired to the nearby bush, resentment painted on his face. He left the next step of the strategy to his mate, observing the situation from a distance.

His partner, the heavier and bigger of the two perched himself on the wing mirror on Peter's side, trying tactics of his own. We did not like that a great deal either, fearing it might not withstand his weight.

'Are you out of your mind', I shouted at the second baboon. He sat very close to Peter who was not as worried as I was.

In response, he lowered his head and peeped onto the three uncooperating occupants of the vehicle. He then pondered what to do next, had no suitable answer and jumped off, indignation written all over his coat.

At last, the cheeky duo had enough, realizing there was nothing for them to get, no snacks, no fees. We waited for them to loose interest as driving on might hurt them. When we did, they looked at us disapprovingly.

Relieved we drove on to the toll booth, which was not occupied by impertinent wayfarers but by friendly staff. For them it was nothing unusual seeing the baboons bothering passing cars. They did not want any snacks, they only collected the fees with a smile.

A cabin at water's edge

For the second time we were at the Storms River Mouth rest camp. This time we stayed overnight in a family cottage with two bedrooms, bathroom and a lounge with a kitchen area. So close to the ocean and surf, the floor of the cabin's verandah was covered in slippery spray.

While my companions went for a walk along the loerie trail, I stayed near the cabin and strolled along the waterfront. The sea surged and frothed. The waves were pounding the rocky shore with great energy. They had broken farther out but were still strong enough to reach the sandy footpath. The surface waves were gradually dissipating between the stones and small rocks. Nothing could be heard except the immense force of the ocean's might.[53]

In the evening, we had a special dinner prepared by the brothers, as Greg was the first to fly back to Europe the following day. To mark the occasion we opened one of the Hamilton Russells, a fitting conclusion to our trip together. With the music of the breakers floating through the cabin walls we drifted off to sleep.

Before we left Storms River the next day we again walked the mondwandelpad. Peter got excited when he discovered a pair of loeries right above our heads on the board walk. With a predominantly green plumage, the birds merged into the canopy and could easily be missed among the foliage. They were busily moving among the branches of the treetops. They were so occupied with whatever they were doing that they did not pay us any attention, and we felt we were not disturbing them in their daily tasks.

After the brief final excursion, we were back on the N2 in a westerly direction.

Through the Cape winelands

Our first goal was George airport, where we arrived two hours later in good time for Greg's departure to Johannesburg and back to Europe. He waved us good bye and walked to check-in for his flight.

Now down to two, I pointed the car back to the road. Our next port of call was 320km from George. Again on a tight schedule, we could not stop anywhere. But at least

---

[53]For details on the functioning of waves see Welland, chapter 5.

we could take the scenic route after Riversdale that meandered along the Langeberg, passing towns like Barrydale,
Montagu and Robertson. The region was well-known for its
farms, orchards and vineyards with their wines and spirits
sought after delicacies. As usual, the towns were named
after some important figure and, also as usual, had a good
number of churches. The mountains were never far away,
so we had splendid views at any time during the drive.

The tough life of settler pioneers

The town of Worcester was our afternoon destination. Surrounded by massive mountain ranges, it welcomed us with
warm sunshine.

The location was one of the places that, in the early
1700s, began to be encroached by Dutch and later by British
settlers. The original occupants of the area, the San and
the Khoi, were soon driven away. By the 1830s, a small
market town had developed that was based on livestock
trading and farming activities. Besides fields and orchards,
another commercial venue had sprung up.

With the Breede River Valley being a wine-producing
region of significance, there were many vineyards. According to *The World Atlas of Wine* more wine is made here
than in most other areas of the Cape. A distillery to make
brandy was established at the end of the 19th century. Governor Cradock, supporting the wine industry, had even introduced the office of Taster for Wines in 1812 in order
to certify the quality of the products. Tempting though it
was, we did not come to visit the wine estates or indeed the
town itself. The local museum was our goal.

In Kleinplasie, just outside Worcester, on the road from
Robertson, we drove to the open air museum commemo-
rating the life of the early pioneer farmers in the Western

Cape. It was due to close at 4:30pm, so we had just one hour to hurry through; we were the only visitors.

The museum covered all aspects of survival at the frontier. There was a tobacco house, a soap kitchen, a water mill, a kraal, a threshing floor, wine cellars, various cottages for labourers and farmers, and a number of other buildings. The floor of the dairy had been made of compacted peach pips. The exhibition hall, in particular, was very instructive. On display were all sorts of farming tools, information on livestock and methods of husbandry, on food production and storage, on transport and about women's share of the workload. Weapons were also shown.

Comparing their basic methods of production with the equipment of modern day agricultural machinery like tractors, mowers, rotators, loaders, balers or ploughs, it is easy to see how hard the daily labours and struggles of those families were. At least, the soil was fertile and rewarded them with good harvests in some of the years.

While hoping for a better life than in their home country, the pioneering settlers must have been iron-willed individuals. They overcame the hardships of climate, disease and toil as well as the resistance of the native tribes, whom they deprived of their hunting and grazing grounds.

So, not able to visit the history museum in Cradock, I now had gained an idea of the settlers' life after all.

Protestant wines

We left Worcester via the R43 for Franschhoek, our evening destination. We came through Villiersdorp a nice little town surrounded by fields and orchards, continuing on the R45. Not going straight on across the Riviersonderend, we turned right and continued along a beautiful lake, the Theewaterskloof Dam. It serves as a water reservoir supplying the surrounding areas and the city of Cape Town. A few baboons sat casually at the kerbside of the road, not taking the slightest notice and not bent on harassing us.

The higher we climbed the mountain, the more the road zigzagged. A vantage point of the pass offered splendid views over the valley of the French Corner. The first Huguenot families had arrived at the end of the 17th century and settled among the Dutch farmers. A great number of them were given land in the area which came to be named after them. Surrounded by high mountain peaks, sheltering the area from strong winds, the settlers established their home in the valley and adjacent plain and soon started profitable vineyards. The region went on to become one of the top wine producing districts in South Africa if not the world.

Residence Klein Oliphants Hoek was on a quiet street of Franschhoek. Once a missionary station dating from 1888, it was an intimate privately-run hotel. The house had lovingly appointed rooms and a warm atmosphere as well as a carefully tended garden.

Before dinner we explored the town, a place popular with tourists. A good number of galleries, coffee shops, hotels, guest houses and wineries reflected its attraction for visitors. The restaurants' menus in particular looked very appealing but we had to turn away from their enticing list of dishes, as we needed to return to the guest house.

We had to be back at the Residence at 8pm sharp for a special dinner with regional game on the menu. The proprietors were a chef and a sommelière serving their house guests only. Since the kitchen staff prepared every meal with great dedication, dinner took over two and a half hours. For each course the appropriate wine was recommended, and we duly tasted what was being offered to us. For dessert we had a red Muscadel, a grape that has been grown at the Cape for centuries. Bursting with fresh fruit flavours, the sweet wine deserved to be appreciated in small amounts only.

Won over by a charming hippo

It was our last day in South Africa. We had to re-arrange our luggage for the flights, safely packing the elephant and the fragile bottles of wine.

Mid morning we left Franschhoek for Cape Town, passing more wine country and mountain landscapes.

Boschendal, near the intersection of R45 and R310, was one of the famous Cape wine estates. Like many other such establishments, it was founded by Huguenots in the late 1600s. The estate's extensive vineyards catered for the world's wine enthusiasts, regrettably we had no more space even for one bottle. Next to the manor house in the Cape Dutch style, there was a large wonderful park, a nice restaurant and a couple of outbuildings. Once family owned, the estate is today managed by a consortium and expanded to more commercial dimensions, ranging from hospitality and accommodation to agriculture and livestock farming and of course winemaking.

On the way back to the car, I briefly popped into the giftshop and a couple of minutes later emerged not with yet another mug but with a captivating hippo. Handmade in South Africa and painted by the artist in a variety of cheerful colours, he sat there waiting for someone to give him a home. Without a moments hesitation, he and I were on friendly terms, and he agreed to exchange his spot in the shop for a place in a house near the woods. His bright colouration made up for his small size, and he now resides far north in the company of the much bigger elephant.

Stellenbosch, another of the old towns that were named after the Cape's governor Simon van der Stel, was South Africa's second oldest town. That would have been a good enough reason to visit. We drove into a few streets around the centre with plenty of Cape Dutch buildings; this way we could get at least an impression of the place.

Located in a hilly region, the town not only had a historic centre but also many wineries around its district, none of which we could visit for lack of time, not even Meerlust Estate that the waiter in Cape Town had recommended. Luckily though, we had a few of their wines well-wrapped in our luggage, but visiting the praised winery would have been an extra treat.

We pressed on to Cape Town Airport, bringing our round trip of almost 3,000km along the southern coast of South Africa to a close.

From grassland to bookshelf

The check-in ladies were slightly confused about our assorted tickets: paper tickets, electronic tickets, economy seats on the domestic flight to Johannesburg, business class seats for the longhaul to London, and tickets bought from more than one source.

With a most colourful bunch of protea flowers in my bag, we were heading back to the UK. Our two African animals travelled safely in the overhead locker above our heads. Floating above the clouds, I hoped they had a trip as comfortable as I had on the airline's luxurious flatbed.

Years later, the flowers have faded, but the elephant and the hippo are still there, contented with their life among our ever growing collection of African books.

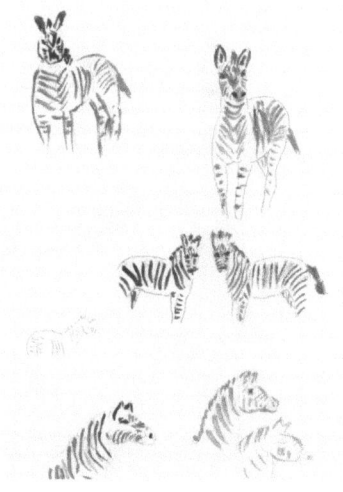

'Allurements which will well repay the
trouble of the journey'

Magic Moments

With my head in my books about the animals, the landscapes, the plants, and the history of southern Africa, I had imagined what it was like to see everything with my own eyes. Reality surpassed my expectations.

Having encountered the animals on the pages, it had been exciting to meet them in their true habitat. Dangerous, capricious or brash, from overbearing baboons to eloquent birds, from tiny beetles to giant elephants, from the smallest to the majestic, we encountered a multitude of characters, anthropomorphized or not. Some ended up on my notepad. And some in our library.

The spectacular landscapes of South Africa and Lesotho, their steep mountains and wide plateaus, savannah and woodlands, semi-desert and coastal strips, offered a richness of unexpected vistas. The plant life from the drought-surviving to the sun-loving proved the versatility and adaptability of the natural world.

Driving through both countries, I felt a sense of the past was lingering everywhere.

I agreed with Anthony Trollope's view that the efforts of travelling foreign lands are worth the excitement and experience gained. The "allurements" were the magic of the wild.[54]

The buffalo horns at the entrance gate to my childhood home seemed to be some kind of mysterious chimera. The animals I encountered as an adult in the African savannah were very much alive and grunting, bellowing, snorting, dozing - and smiling.

---

[54]South Africa, vol I, p75.

Authors and Titles

Bibliography

Barrow John, An account of travels into the interior of southern Africa in the year 1797 and 1798. Two volumes. T. Cadell, London 1801, 1804

Behrendt Stephen D., Latham A.J.H., Northrup David, The diary of Antera Duke, an eighteenth-century African slave trader. Oxford University Press, New York 2010

Bowen Huw V., McAleer John, Blyth Robert J., Monsoon traders. The maritime world of the East India Company. Scala Publishers, London 2011

Borschberg Peter ed., Journal, memorials and letters of Cornelis Matelieff de Jonge. Security, diplomacy and commerce in 17th-century Southeast Asia. NUS Press, Singapore 2016

Bryden Bruce, A game ranger remembers. Jonathan Ball Publishers, Johannesburg and Cape Town 2010

Burchell William John, Travels in the interior of southern Africa. Two volumes. Longman, London 1822, 1824

Casalis Eugène, The Basutos or twenty-three years in South Africa. James Nisbet, London 1861

Compton Robert Harold, Kirstenbosch - Garden for a nation. Tafelberg Uitgewers, Cape Town 1965

Corn Charles, The scents of Eden. A history of the spice trade. Kodansha America, New York 1999

Danziger Christopher, A trader's century. The fortunes of Frasers. Purnell & Sons, Cape Town 1979

Douglas-Hamilton Iain and Oria, Among the elephants. Collins & Harvill Press, London 1975

Earl Lawrence, Crocodile fever. A true story of adventure. Collins, London 1954

Fell R.T., Early maps of South-East Asia. Oxford University Press, Singapore 1991

Fitzpatrick Percy, Jock of the Bushveld. Longmans, Green and Co., London 1907

Fransen Hans, Cook Mary, The old buildings of the Cape. Balkema, Cape Town 1980

Gaastra Femme Simon, The Dutch East India Company. Expansion and decline. Walburg Pers, Zutphen 2003

Gill Stephen J., A short history of Lesotho. From the late stone age until the 1993 election. Morija Museum and Archives, Morija 1993

Gribbin John and Mary, Flower hunters. Oxford University Press, New York 2008

Gurnah Abdulrazak, Paradise. Hamish Hamilton, London 1994

Harding Richard, Seapower and naval warfare 1650-1830. Unniversity College London Press, London 1999

Hazell Alastair, The last slave market. The incredible story of John Kirk: the man who ended the East African slave trade. Constable, London 2012

Johnson Hugh, Robinson Jancis, The World Atlas of Wine. Octopus Publishing Group, London 2003

Keegan Timothy, Colonial South Africa and the origins of the racial order. Leicester University Press, London 1996

Kendall Kathryn Limakatso ed., Basali ! Stories by and about women in Lesotho. University of Natal Press, Pietermaritzburg 1995

Kendall Kathryn Limakatso ed., Singing away the hunger. Stories of a life in Lesotho. University of Natal Press, Pietermaritzburg 1996

Kipling Rudyard, Just so stories. Macmillan, London 1966

Kruger Kobie, The wilderness family. At home with Africa's wildlife. Bantam Books, Transworld Publishers, London 2002

Leakey Richard, Morell Virginia, Wildlife wars. My fight to save Africa's natural treasures. St. Martin's Press, New York 2001

Mandela Nelson, Long walk to Freedom. Abacus, London 2004

Masson Francis, An Account of Three Journeys from the Cape Town into the Southern Parts of Africa; Undertaken for the Discovery of New Plants, towards the Improvement of the Royal Botanical Gardens at Kew. By Mr. Francis Masson, One of His Majesty's Gardeners. Addressed to Sir John Pringle, Bart. P.R.S., vol 66, p268-317, Philosophical Transactions of the Royal Society, London January 1776 (royalsocietypublishing.org)

Matthews Barbara, The man they called Vukani. The life and times of Harold Trollope. Bluecliff Publishing, Port Elizabeth 2005

Owens Delia and Mark, Cry of the Kalahari. Collins, London 1985

Patterson Gareth, The secret elephants. The rediscovery of the world's most southerly elephants. Penguin Books, Johannesburg 2011

Payne Katy, Silent thunder. The hidden voice of elephants. Weidenfeld & Nicolson, London 1998

Paynter David, Nussey Wilf, Kruger - Portrait of a National Park. Macmillan, Johannesburg 1986

Pelúcia Alexandra, Corsários e piratas Portugueses. Aventureiros nos mares da Ásia. A esfera dos livros, Lisboa 2010

Percival Robert, An account of the Cape of Good Hope. Reprint edition 1804. Negro Universities Press, New York 1969

Prak Maarten, The Dutch Republic in the seventeenth century. The Golden Age. Cambridge University Press, New York 2009

Prince William of Sweden, Among Pygmies and Gorillas. With the Swedish Zoological Expedition to Central Africa in 1921. Gyldenval, Copenhagen 1923

Raven-Hart Rowland, Before van Riebeeck. Callers at South Africa from 1488-1652. C. Struik Publishers, Cape Town 1967

Robinson Jancis, Confessions of a wine lover. Viking, London 1997

Schreiner Olive, The story of an African farm. Oxford University Press, Oxford 1992

Shell Robert, Children of bondage. A social history of the slave society at the Cape of Good Hope, 1652-1838. Wesleyan University Press, Hanover, NH 1994

Stevenson-Hamilton James, South African Eden. From Sabi Game Reserve to Kruger National Park. Collins, London 1974

The Oriental Navigator, or, New directions for sailing to and from the East Indies, China, New Holland. London 1801

Thom Hendrik Bernardus ed., Journal of Jan van Riebeeck. Three volumes. Van Riebeeck Society, Cape Town 1952-1958

Throckmorton Peter ed., The sea remembers. Shipwrecks and archaeology. Artists House, London 1987

Tooley Ronald Vere, Maps and map-makers. B.T. Batsford Ltd., London 1961

Trollope Anthony, South Africa. Two volumes. Reprint edition 1878. Nonsuch Publishing, Stroud 2005

Van der Post Laurens, The heart of the hunter. Vintage, London 2002

Van der Post Laurens, The lost world of the Kalahari. Penguin, London 1962

Van Warmelo Nicolaas Jacobus, Place names of the Kruger National Park Republic of South Africa. Department of Bantu Administration. Ethnological Publication No 47. The Government Printer, Pretoria 1961

Van Wyk Piet, Field guide to the trees of the Kruger National Park. C. Struik Publishers, Cape Town 1984

Wallis John Peter Richard. Thomas Baines. His life and explorations in South Africa, Rhodesia and Australia. 1820-1875. A.A. Balkema, Rotterdam 1976

Watson Lyall, Elephantoms. Tracking the elephant. Norton & Company, New York 2002

Welland Michael, Sand. A journey through science and the imagination. Oxford University Press, New York 2009

Wolhuter Harry, Memories of a game ranger. Collins/ Fontana Books, London 1973